THE
ANYWHERE LEADER

THE
ANYWHERE LEADER

How to Lead and Succeed in Any Business Environment

Mike Thompson

JOSSEY-BASS
A Wiley Imprint
www.josseybass.com

Published by Jossey-Bass
A Wiley Imprint
989 Market Street, San Francisco, CA 94103-1741—www.josseybass.com

Radical Sabbatical™ is a registered trademark of SVI, LLC.

Readers should be aware that Internet websites offered as citations and/or sources for
further information may have changed or disappeared between the time this was written
and when it is read.

Limit of Liability/Disclaimer of Warranty: While the publisher and author have used
their best efforts in preparing this book, they make no representations or warranties with
respect to the accuracy or completeness of the contents of this book and specifically
disclaim any implied warranties of merchantability or fitness for a particular purpose. No
warranty may be created or extended by sales representatives or written sales materials.
The advice and strategies contained herein may not be suitable for your situation. You
should consult with a professional where appropriate. Neither the publisher nor author
shall be liable for any loss of profit or any other commercial damages, including but not
limited to special, incidental, consequential, or other damages.

Jossey-Bass books and products are available through most bookstores. To contact Jossey-
Bass directly call our Customer Care Department within the U.S. at 800-956-7739,
outside the U.S. at 317-572-3986, or fax 317-572-4002.

Jossey-Bass also publishes its books in a variety of electronic formats. Some content that
appears in print may not be available in electronic books.

Library of Congress Cataloging-in-Publication Data

Thompson, Mike.
    The anywhere leader: how to lead and succeed in any business environment / Mike
Thompson.—1st ed.
        p.   cm.
    Includes index.
    ISBN 978-1-118-00234-6 (cloth); ISBN 978-1-118-08454-0 (ebk); ISBN 978-1-118-
08455-7 (ebk); ISBN 978-1-118-08456-4 (ebk)
    1. Leadership.   2. Executive ability.   I. Title.
    HD57.7.T46736   2011
    658.4'092—dc23

                                                                    2011021321

Printed in the United States of America
FIRST EDITION
HB Printing   10 9 8 7 6 5 4 3 2 1

CONTENTS

To my dad, Terry Thompson,
for showing me the world below the sun and the life above it.

Part One

INTRODUCTION TO THE ANYWHERE LEADER

THE ANYWHERE LEADER

Instability and change are nothing new. John F. Kennedy said, "The one unchangeable certainty is that nothing is certain or unchangeable." But those words seem especially relevant in the second decade of the twenty-first century. A severe recession, high-tech bubble, real estate bubble, the crash of those bubbles, tough global competition for low-wage jobs, and aggressive cross-border deal-making have all changed the status quo for businesses and employees. Managers manage crisis to crisis, day to day, quarter to quarter. Long-term goals keep receding into the distance. People wonder how trade wars, unemployment, and partisan bickering will change their employment and economic security. They want to know how to adapt to tough new rules of a progressive yet turbulent universe where people are misplaced, replaced, and displaced.

Anyone in business today must be able to lead through uncertainty and disruption. He must become that person who lands on his feet and moves forward no matter what the setting or situation presents. He must become what I call an Anywhere Leader.

As the CEO of an organizational development firm called SVI, I have seen first-hand the business landscape turn upside down in recent years—and business leaders scramble to keep up. The power structure has changed entirely. In the global economy, research and development is no longer limited to the corporate headquarters. Ideas are coming from the field because companies are collaborating with their markets and their communities much more than with the central office. Power is not centralized, but distributed. In other words, Headquarters has lost a large amount of its punch; it has been replaced by conversations in all corners of the globe, generating new ideas and new growth. Change definitely brings opportunity. But it can also bring an entire organization to its knees.

Over the past decade, I've been immersed in the research and study of leadership. In the course of my work—after thousands of interactions, interviews, and observations—I've found that the managers who have advanced their careers through tumultuous times are the ones who find a way to fit in, build trust, and contribute quickly in any setting in which they are placed.

The Anywhere Leader was partly inspired by first-hand experience. My team and I work with some of the world's largest and most complex companies. We're asked to help them build talent, solve managerial problems, increase organizational productivity, provide talent development systems and tools, and assess organizational and leadership effectiveness. In any given week, we may be immersed in ten different initiatives at ten different companies with ten distinctive corporate cultures.

SVI has a distinctive culture, as well—one that is entirely comfortable and familiar to me. But in order to succeed, I have to be able to land in any one of those other corporate environments and quickly understand how things get done there. The same holds true for any manager or business owner striving to succeed in a market where collaboration and worldwide understanding are key. When our team works with multiple clients, it's clear that we'll be highly ineffective unless we can navigate well across many different work environments, structures, standards, expected behaviors, rules, routines, and norms.

In fact, the only time I've been fired from a client was when I failed to recognize their culture—and therefore failed to behave in an acceptable and productive manner. I came into that organization like a bull blindly charging forward, with little concern for anything but my own ego. I had no curiosity, wrong motives, and lots of wrong assumptions. And because of this, my perspective was off and my advice was dead wrong.

Anywhere Leaders don't make such mistakes. Those highly adaptable and resourceful leaders easily navigate and succeed wherever they find themselves, and that is their profound advantage.

I wasn't supposed to be a businessman. I was supposed to be the next Chuck Yeager, breaking bounds as a test pilot. That's why I started my career in the Air Force, not in a corporation. The Air Force gave me some intense training, but none as extreme as Survival and Tactical Evasion training in Spokane, Washington . . . in December. Over seventeen days, I learned how to hide, find water, signal for help, stay warm, identify safe areas, cover my tracks, and set traps. I was trained to survive in the harshest, most unfamiliar (to say the least) environment, and I thought I was doing pretty well—until my comrades and I were captured and taken to a "prisoner of war camp."

Not quite the desired result, but what I learned from that exercise, and from the military in general, was how to navigate the unknown. I learned how to adapt to new terrain and the challenges it presents. I discovered that if you want to survive, you must be aware of your surroundings, know what personalities you're dealing with (that is, who can help you and who's going to stab you in the back with a bayonet), and be amazingly resourceful. You can't throw anything away, because everything could be a valuable tool. It was incredible training that I'll never forget. But what I didn't realize back then was how vital those skills would become to surviving in today's business world—one of the harshest environments around.

To succeed in our turbulent economy, you've got to become a leader who can land in foreign territory, fit right in, and immediately contribute—moving the work forward using whatever tools are available to you. You have to be able to put progress over politics and be open to new ideas. Those leaders who can't adapt and drive progress—who resist new ideas, lack social savvy, and are afraid to take risks—lose their relevance and edge.

Take Thomas, for example. He's a director of product development for a worldwide consumer packaged goods company. Thomas has achieved superstar status in his organization as an "idea guy" and has had an incredible twelve-year run, with one success followed by another. In fact, under his leadership, his company launched two new product lines that have generated double-digit growth in market share.

Thomas has become very comfortable with his role, and he knows how business is done in his organization. You might say he's cracked the code—showing up at the right meetings, using the right resources, getting involved in the right projects, and making the right promises. He's savvy, too. He looks good, presents well, and can easily dial up the humor when necessary. He's got lots of promise, his team is the best in the company, and his career path looks strong.

Except for one thing.

Thomas isn't an Anywhere Leader. He may be successful in his current work environment, but drop him down in Brazil, put him in with a team of Millennials, or have him lead a newly acquired company, and he'll sink. Why? Because although Thomas excels at what he knows, he lacks the necessary traits to lead in the unknown and in the uncertainty. Success in a familiar environment, with familiar people and a familiar product, doesn't equate to success in new territory—whether it's down the hall, across the country, or halfway around the world. For Thomas to open up more career opportunities for himself, he's going to have to spread his influence and succeed beyond the work that's familiar to him. He needs to broaden his experience so that he can mirror, on a personal level, the worldwide mindset and contribution of his organization. Because his company operates cross-culturally, Thomas will have to lead cross-culturally in order to advance.

Beth is a different story. She's already found herself in unfamiliar territory—and she's not happy to be there. Beth leads a team that has been dramatically downsized, from twenty-five people to just five, following her company's merger with a competitor. Sure, the merger will bring a few new people to the team to help out with capacity, but everyone will be asked to do a lot more with a lot less. And there's bound to be some animosity with the newbies— after all, up until now they were the competition. Beth has very little confidence in this new direction. She's against it—in fact, she feels like the company is making a big mistake.

Beth has a couple of choices in how she responds to this shift. She can either resist the change or commit to it. If she resists, her career with the company will likely be short-lived. After all, plenty of others would be happy to take her job. For as long as she remains in her job, her resistance will surely be unproductive—if not downright destructive. But if Beth were to develop the traits of an Anywhere Leader, she could help her newly formed team move beyond animosity toward camaraderie. By bringing an exploratory mindset and a passion for progress, Beth would build trust. She'd become a go-to leader, which would escalate her career. Beth's response to the situation is her choice, but adopting *anywhere* tendencies would turn a tough circumstance into a valuable opportunity for Beth, for her team, and for her organization.

The Anywhere Leader is for Thomas and Beth and every manager who needs to develop the traits that will allow them to lead—and succeed—in any business environment. It gives leaders the insight and skills to take their career to the next level, no matter where they are. Anywhere Leaders are effective managers to begin with. Like Thomas and Beth, they've had a good track record of success at whatever level in the organization they are placed. But unlike Thomas and Beth, they have also developed core traits and behaviors that help them successfully lead in work environments and cultures that may be quite foreign to them.

So just who is this business champion? He's a highly regarded, chameleon-like manager or independent professional who can change his colors and adjust his approach without losing his identity. Anywhere Leaders are socially savvy and sensationally curious. They rarely envy the success of others—quite the contrary. They're content with their position and inspired by anyone's success. But don't misinterpret their sense of ease and genuine good nature for a lack of drive. Their drive sets them apart.

He's Kent Thiry, a health care executive who was ninety days away from a well-deserved and much-anticipated retirement when he was asked to interview for the top job at Total Renal Care (TRC)—a company dealing with enormous disruption and uncertainty. This nationwide kidney dialysis provider could barely make payroll at the time and was experiencing a mass exodus of executive talent. Fast-forward ten years. Kent is still far from retirement. His talent for uniting individuals under hard times, crafting an engaging culture, and eradicating cynicism through lead-by-example honesty transformed that company from a two-months-from-failure cautionary tale to a textbook example of turnaround. Now renamed DaVita ("to give life" in Italian—a name picked by TRC employees), Kent's organization stands as a leader in the industry. What makes Kent an Anywhere Leader? He had the ability to succeed through disruption and ignite a culture because of his drive for progress.

She's Anne Livermore, who saw that HP was lagging behind its competition and decided that the best way to regain lost ground was to buck its legendary (and loved) decentralized culture. Today she serves as executive vice president of HP's Enterprise Business—the division that consolidates and aligns HP's hardware, software, and service solutions to customer needs. But bucking trends (and being right) isn't all it takes to be an Anywhere Leader. Although many would say that Anne's success stems from her ability to make quick decisions and foresee industry trends, her Anywhere Leader status comes from her commitment to the organization above the other compelling opportunities. Despite thrice being shortlisted by industry experts as next in line for the executive office, yet being passed over for outsiders, Anne remains ardently committed to HP—what it stands for and what it can be for its customers. In a world where organizational interests take second place to career advancement, her values-centric leadership style and sheer determination make her definite Anywhere Leader material.

He's Donnie Smith, who led the turnaround at Tyson Foods by inspiring a culture where everyone has a voice and everyone participates. Donnie knows how to leverage an entire organization. Even as the CEO of one of the world's largest protein providers, Donnie is extremely open and inclusive, using every relationship, every resource, and any idea to improve the business. His ability to connect with others and push for improvement makes him extremely resourceful, as he uses every component of Tyson to attain business excellence.

These Anywhere Leaders have distinctive styles and missions, but they share one critical skill: the ability to adapt to, and broker, positive change in any environment.

To carry out such positive change in any environment, the Anywhere Leader has developed three core traits. These traits are depicted in Figure 1.1.

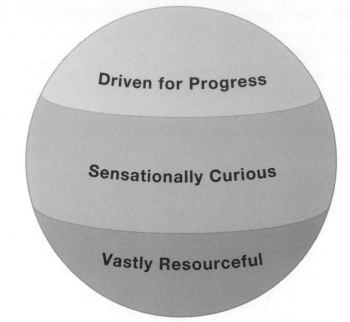

Figure 1.1 Three Core Traits of the Anywhere Leader

Driven for Progress

The Anywhere Leader succeeds because he's driven more by the push for progress than by politics.

What's the value of playing politics in a world where things are hardly stable, where connections are temporary, and where ideas race through their lifecycle at record speed? The Anywhere Leader's loyalty is to the work. He operates within established processes, but will defend the progress, not the party line.

I'm always impressed when politicians are bold enough to cross party lines behind an idea. As I wrote in my previous book, *The Organizational Champion*: ". . . champions will occasionally transcend partisan perceptions and move forward even under the most extreme circumstances. Who shook Gorbachev's hand in Reykjavik? 'Archconservative hawk' Ronald Reagan. Who signed the first legislation to seriously rein in welfare? 'Bleeding-heart liberal' Bill

Clinton." In those moments, these leaders' drive for progress bridged entrenched ideological rifts. They were willing to inflame the anger of their supporters by making decisions that did not yield short-term benefits but would contribute to big-picture goals such as nuclear disarmament and economic growth.

The Anywhere Leader earns respect from his team because he will move in front of an initiative before the initiative has been fully proven or embraced by others. Although others are hesitant to adopt an idea before they understand its impact on their image, the Anywhere Leader is an early adopter of a great idea—and therefore willing to champion the idea and the people who came up with it.

Bill and Bob Gore are examples of Anywhere Leaders who championed great ideas before they actually got legs. If you're familiar with GORE-TEX, then you should know this father-and-son duo. They invented it. When no one else—including his own employer, DuPont—believed in the utility of plastics and the wide potential for its use, Bill left to start his own company to explore the possibilities. The rest is history. Today, GORE-TEX is a leading product in the outdoor wear category. But few know that the Gores are also behind today's smoother, nonshredding, plastics-based dental floss. Bill Gore loved this dental floss because it didn't hurt his gums. Others, including Johnson & Johnson and Colgate-Palmolive, felt like consumers wouldn't buy it because, at the time, everyone believed that dental floss *should* hurt. If it didn't, people thought that it just wasn't working. I'm glad the Gores championed their ideas despite criticism and resistance from the industries. So are my gums. The Gores weren't working to win a popularity contest. They were working to drive progress. Like all Anywhere Leaders, they were aware of the business opportunities and in tune with the work at hand. People want to work with progress-minded leaders who champion great ideas without bending under the pressure from perceived experts. That's why these leaders are trusted wherever they go.

Being progress-driven brings with it a set of related strengths. We'll get into them in greater detail in later chapters, but in a nutshell, our research shows that Anywhere Leaders who are driven toward progress are *discerning, daring,* and *determined.* Fueled by those characteristics, Anywhere Leaders know what's valuable and worth pursuing, and what's a big waste of time. They are resilient in the face of setbacks, determined to press on and succeed. And they are not afraid to take chances and fail—even when the stakes are high—because the work is right and good.

Anywhere Leaders may be all about the work, but their drive for progress has the added benefit of being hugely motivating to the people around them. When you mix discernment, a willingness to dare, and determination, you get a leader who stirs change within a team or organization. People trust a leader who knows right from wrong, who commits to the right in spite of potential consequences. The Anywhere Leader fuels this charge because he remains engaged and passionate despite the barriers. He makes a lasting impact on the business because his bold moves create competitive advantages and change the game in his company's favor.

Sensationally Curious

It's interesting how, as a society, we think about curiosity. We don't like our kids asking "Why?" five times in a row when we tell them to "get away from that." In an office environment, it isn't uncommon to hear, "Don't question it; that's just the way we do things around here." Curiosity is a vital trait that many view as annoying—even dangerous. The saying goes that curiosity killed the cat . . . but as far as I know, cats always land on their feet. And because the Anywhere Leader's curiosity leads to valuable insights and understanding, she lands on her feet as well.

Thinking about today's business landscape: many companies are so desperate to keep up with rapid change that they blindly rush into new initiatives and processes—bullishly believing that it's the only way to go. But if you lack curiosity—and the understanding that comes from it—the only change you're likely to see is increasing irrelevancy for both you and your company. Panic leads organizations and managers to make changes for the sake of change, without any insight behind it. The desperate leader says, "Something's wrong—quick, do something—anything." The Anywhere Leader asks, "What's wrong? Where did the problem begin? And how did we get here?"

I recently had the opportunity to observe an emergency room and see how doctors and nurses respond to critically ill patients with dire prognoses. I learned that even in the most extreme circumstances, the critical care team's first response is to assess, not to act. A wrong move would only make things worse. The right move would make all the difference toward a hopeful recovery. In an emergency room, quick and decisive actions save lives, but understanding the issues is the crucial starting point. Why do we want our doctors to be curious about our illness, understanding of our history, and aware of our vitals, but we want our employees to go straight to the answers—to the solutions? Like the ER doc, the Anywhere Leader assesses before acting—which is why her actions are usually productive.

Curious leaders would rather pose the right questions that give them a deeper understanding than compete to deliver answers in hopes of acknowledgment. Curiosity allows the Anywhere Leader to adopt an exploratory mindset in everything she does. When she finds herself in a new role or leading a new team, she's quick to gain meaningful insight into the people around her, the organizational culture, and the processes of the business. And she's able to discover and maximize all available resources. She starts by asking who, what, where, when, and how—not by stating new ground rules and implementing new procedures right out of the gate.

Sensationally curious leaders have the additional strengths of being *reflective*, *receptive*, and *perceptive*. They're able to dissect any issue and get to its core because they keep asking themselves—and others—that vital question: "Why?" Being open to new ideas allows them to seek and use the insights of others to make progress. And because they observe people and processes, they have a deeper understanding of the situations they're in. Curious leaders use their reflection, reception, and perception to tackle challenges head-on.

Vastly Resourceful

In addition to curiosity, the Anywhere Leader is successful because he's *vastly resourceful*. Resourcefulness is an essential trait of the Anywhere Leader because it means he can do a lot with a little—or a lot with a lot. Some of you may recall the TV series *MacGyver*, back in the '80s. (If you missed it, you might know the spoof *MacGruber*, a recent *Saturday Night Live* sketch turned movie.) The series features a cool and collected secret agent who is constantly facing life-threatening challenges. Normally he has only a few seconds to find a solution, or he and whoever else is with him are toast. In every tight spot, MacGyver finds whatever tool is readily available to him—a rubber band, a paper clip, a pencil—and in a matter of seconds figures out how to turn it into a lifesaver. He takes the rubber band and uses it to tie knots, lock doors, create a diversion, whatever. The point is that MacGyver is resourceful. He can do amazing things with only a few items.

Like MacGyver, the Anywhere Leader can look at a tool, an opportunity, or an issue and see much more than most people can. He looks at things more deeply. When a psychologist puts a picture of an ink blot in front of him and asks what he sees, the Anywhere Leader comes up with a pretty exhaustive list. This trait lets him successfully shift from places where resources are abundant, budgets are big, and information is plentiful to more challenging areas where resources are greatly limited. Good thing, too, because that's an increasingly common scenario these days.

A brand manager from Chicago may have a multimillion-dollar budget to work with to drive consumer interest, but later may be asked to lead a recently launched product line that has only a sliver of that amount. Imagine yourself in that situation. You've successfully increased market share with your company's primary product. In fact, you did too good a job, because now your company wants you to do the same thing with a struggling product that has faltered practically from its launch. Your reward for a job well done in your previous assignment is a shoestring budget, an untested and randomly organized team, and an incredibly tough uphill battle to turn a profit with an unproven product. What are you going to do when such a shift happens? Will you obsess about how unfair the situation is and how you deserve better, or will you be resourceful with what you've got in order to achieve greater success?

Just as the Driven for Progress and Sensationally Curious traits have related strengths, so does the Vastly Resourceful trait. Resourceful leaders are *imaginative, inclusive,* and *inventive.* They don't get stuck when the cards are stacked against them. Instead, they're off putting together resources and thinking up their next move so they can get themselves unstuck. They don't quit when the burden increases. Because of their imagination, they can capture those "Aha!" ideas and think up some pretty cool solutions. Inventive leaders also don't mind tinkering. They're comfortable in their "laboratories," testing idea after idea until a "Eureka!" moment strikes. But they don't operate alone; they assemble teams of smart, capable people with diverse backgrounds. Their labs are very collaborative and inclusive environments where ideas abound and progress—not a self-serving agenda—is the priority.

The Anywhere Leader's resourcefulness allows him to get more out of whatever he has to work with—and to stretch it further than most people could ever have imagined. It gives him the edge over others when leading new and less-than-established initiatives, or when he's asked to rescue a sinking ship when everyone else has already bailed. This potent combination of strengths behind their resourcefulness gives Anywhere Leaders resolve. When others quit, they don't. They are able to see the plan through even when things get tough.

Some managers start out with Anywhere Leader characteristics, but lose them once they become successful in a given environment. Thomas, the director of product development we met earlier in the chapter, is a perfect example. Because he's worked in the familiar for so long, his curiosity has atrophied. Convinced that he knows his work, he has stopped asking questions. He's become more charged by personal ambition than by progress. Moreover, Thomas's group is profitable and has money to spend. So Thomas rarely, if ever, does without. If something doesn't work out initially, he just throws more resources at it until the initiative takes flight. A new role in a new work environment would truly be a rude awakening for Thomas. But that's exactly what he needs in order to move forward.

The Anywhere Leader gives managers like Thomas and Beth the tools they need to make that leap. My first book, *The Organizational Champion*, described how our concept of leadership often seems outdated, given the complexities of our times. It emphasized the core principles of a company champion—enlightened and connected change-makers who are opportunity-minded. *The Anywhere Leader* offers additional ideas and insights that reflect the increasing uncertainty under which leaders are expected to operate. To that end, *The Anywhere Leader* seeks to answer these key questions:

- Who are the most effective and successful leaders for today's business environment?

- How can you be an effective leader in unstable business environments?

- How can you drive progress in uncertain times?

- How can you develop the key traits and supporting
  strengths that help you advance your career in today's
  business landscape?

- What effect can you have on your organization by
  being an Anywhere Leader?

To answer these questions, my team at SVI launched a research campaign to understand what type of leaders companies want today and to determine what advantages these leaders bring to their organizations and what traits and strengths are necessary for those leaders to develop.

We quickly learned that the Anywhere Leader concept is both critical to the state of the business in this era and relevant for leaders from corporate conglomerates to sole proprietor start-ups.

We found that companies need to build leaders who are transportable—ones who can move, adjust, take on new challenges, and work in the unfamiliar and the uncertain. As businesses expand and grow, they need leaders with a broad base of skills, who can champion a new charge, ignite a struggling culture, build high-performance teams, sell the business, and create efficiency in operations. Talk about a challenge!

As we conducted our research, we weren't looking for that one person on the planet who had it all—every good leadership quality (all five hundred of them). And we certainly weren't looking to discourage specialization. After all, we need those people who have an exceptional skill in a particular area. But what we hoped our research would prove—and it did—is that a set of learned traits can help anyone adapt to change and influence progress in any environment according to various needs. So although you may not be the most operationally sound leader, you can develop the traits that will help you move an organization to become more operationally sound. You may not be the most visionary person, but you can inspire a team to envision a compelling future. And even if you're not the most creative individual, you can spark the creative drive in others.

Are you this type of leader—an Anywhere Leader? Are you one who can adapt to any business environment and meet any challenge? If your goal is to thrive in the new world, you'll need to develop these key traits of being driven for progress, sensationally curious, and vastly resourceful. You'll need to understand what they represent and how to act in order to use them to their fullest advantage. The following chapters will help you increase your ability to contribute, influence and succeed anywhere, anytime. They'll help you become the Anywhere Leader that today's business demands.

2

THE ANYWHERE LEADER ADVANTAGE

Back in the old days (aka ten years ago), the biggest menace that most business leaders faced was offshoring. Today everyone from senior managers to CEOs to small business owners is starring in a virtual horror flick of his own—with monsters hiding behind every corner ready to leap out and attack. The monsters they know—fickle consumers, fierce competition, and federal regulation—are bad enough. Even scarier are the ones they can't imagine or anticipate. That's what keeps leaders awake at night: the unknown terrors. The next massive oil leak. Rogue public smear campaigns. A terrorist attack in a crowded marketplace. An important investor (or, heaven forbid, a partner) disappearing in the middle of the night. Bird flu, swine flu . . . equestrian flu, anyone? But every good monster story has a hero—and in business, it's the Anywhere Leader.

For too long, we've been developing our business leaders to defend against the predictable. There's no such thing anymore.

Even the most successful companies and seasoned managers can't rely on yesterday's strategies; our global business environment is just too volatile. Many will learn the hard way that a storied past has little bearing on the present—and none whatsoever on the future. Anywhere Leaders know that in order to soar ahead, you don't look back. And they have a distinct advantage because of it.

Anywhere Leaders Drive Progress

South Africa's hero was Nelson Mandela. No one would have blamed Mandela for looking back on the injustice and tyranny he experienced. He chose to look forward. Whether you like his politics or not, Mandela brought progress and reconciliation to a nation that was organized by apartheid, racism, violence, and oppression. Once Mandela was released in 1990 from a South African prison after twenty-seven years, he quickly grew in power within his party, the African National Congress (ANC). The ANC has been the dominant political party in South Africa since 1994, the year Mandela won the South African presidency. With Mandela in charge, ANC members were eager for the political power play behind the ANC agenda.

But like other Anywhere Leaders, Mandela's priority was progress, not politics. Mandela knew that for the betterment of South Africa, he was going to have to be the symbol for reconciliation in a nation that was highly diverse, highly segregated, and battling an array of serious social issues. Mandela reached across party lines to connect the nation and inspire a new love of country. His ability to connect and inspire love was captured in the 2009 movie *Invictus*. The film featured Mandela's enthusiasm and support for the South African rugby team, the Springboks. In 1995, the Springboks were serious underdogs to win the World Cup, even though South Africa, labeled the "Rainbow Nation," was hosting the tournament. Against significant odds, the Rainbow Nation's Springboks defeated New Zealand's All-Blacks. In a gesture that was widely seen as a major step toward reconciliation between white and black South Africans, Mandela presented the Rugby World Cup Trophy to the white South African rugby team captain, Francois Pienaar, while wearing his jersey.

Anywhere Leaders' Broad-Based Skills Build Organizational Agility

Anywhere Leaders are the business heroes for the twenty-first century because they inspire and enable progress. They're nimble adversaries, with the broadest talents and skills and the best chance of defending against surprise threats. Anywhere Leaders aren't motivated by personal gain, but their skills and mindset sure put them in line for it. They have a distinct advantage over other managers who don't have their resolve, adaptability, power to motivate, and ability to connect with others. Those skills help their organizations become more agile, help them achieve significant personal and professional growth, and make them prime candidates for promotion and career advancement.

Compare the highly specialized leader in your organization with the one who has a very broad base of skills. Today, as leaders climb the career ladder, those with the broadest skill base get further. Why? Because our unpredictable challenges call for leaders who can think on their feet and apply any number of skills to any number of problems. Compare the leader who thrives in a defined and predictable process to the leader who can function when things aren't black and white, but very gray. Today's uncertain business environments demand leaders who can operate when the answers aren't perfectly clear. Compare the frustrated leader whose first reaction following failure is to find someone to fire with the leader who enables the success of a struggling employee while demanding personal accountability for results. That's the kind of person successful companies are searching for to lead their businesses in the twenty-first century.

Anywhere Leaders Ignite Performance Cultures

Being an Anywhere Leader creates multiple career opportunities because it makes you the go-to person for compelling assignments. As an Anywhere Leader, you're often placed in high-growth or problem areas because you're able to ignite cultures. You can take high-turnover, low-production cultures and create a sense of purpose and camaraderie that ushers in a new level of commitment to performance. Your boss, colleagues, clients, and customers all know that you can fit in anywhere, adapt to any change, and show results with whatever resources are available to you. And the more opportunities you have, the broader your skills and understanding become. You're exposed to more things and you gain new perspective, deepen and widen your relationships, and increase your likeability and respect.

Like Mandela, Anywhere Leaders can bring unity and reconciliation to toxic cultures because they ignite a spirit of resolve and a new commitment to progress. Mandela has the ability to relate, to be empathetic, and to be socially attuned. And these abilities helped him bring new hope to communities and cultures that didn't have much of a reason to hope. Such abilities help leaders like Mandela to build necessary trust and gain confidence from their followers.

Having Anywhere Leader traits puts you on a path of discovery when it comes to business initiatives, too. Being driven for progress helps you uncover new markets and growth areas. Being curious leads you to new approaches and solutions where you might never have found them before. And being resourceful allows you to create and advance projects and initiatives that are sustainable, despite limitations or setbacks.

Anywhere Leaders Turn Madness into Brilliance

"A bigger plane will never be built." That bold statement came from a Boeing engineer in 1933 following the launch of the "new"

Boeing 247. The 247 was the first of its kind, boasting many technical and aerodynamic advances. It introduced a higher level of safety to the industry because it was the first two-engine aircraft that could fly on just one engine—a valuable feature considering how unreliable engines were back then.

You can't blame that engineer for being excited, but his statement is a Hall of Famer in the bad predictions category and in narrow-mindedness. The 247 held only ten passengers. Just fourteen years later, the sometimes maddening, sometimes brilliant, and always daring Howard Hughes successfully flew his five-story-high and football field–wide H-4 Hercules heavy transport aircraft for the first time. Today's jumbo jets, including Boeing's own 747, can carry over five hundred passengers. Though Howard Hughes was no Anywhere Leader—he was, after all, insane—I have to give him credit for being a daring visionary. Hughes saw the many possibilities that others couldn't. If only he had been more practical in how he pursued them, his legacy might not have been so tarnished and we might focus more on his brilliance than we do on his madness.

Unlike Hughes, Amazon.com's founder and CEO, Jeff Bezos, is an Anywhere Leader because he attaches discernment and determination to his daring pursuits. Most of us who have studied Bezos quickly acknowledge his micromanagement style and frugality and his extreme desire to keep from conforming. He's also a "root-cause analysis" guy who asks "Why?" a lot to get to the bottom of things. So let's get to the root of his management style—the *deeper felt need* (below the surface) aspect of his leadership behavior—which he emphasizes more than his skill. It might seem fairly bold of me to infer all this about Bezos's personal and inward drive. You may be wondering how I can form such a conclusion. If you haven't already, I encourage you to read his 2010 commencement speech to Princeton University. In it, Bezos gets fairly personal and recounts the importance and impact of his life choices. You'll realize that Bezos is guided by integrity and by a desire to do the good and right things. Bezos is a passionate person who loves the emotional connection to a grand purpose or a cause or a mission—and he loves adventure. He's an original who likes original things. He's authentic, driven for progress and driven by the rightness of the work. Because his motives stem from his core rather than from a need to impress business experts, people trust his decisions—and the discernment behind his drive for progress has enabled Bezos to reinvent retail.

Reinvent retail? How so?

Bezos emphasized market share over profits to grow Amazon .com, and a broad consumer target for his online retail format. According to the Academy of Achievement, Bezos wanted to replace the "Earth's biggest bookstore" brand association with the "Earth's biggest anything store." A few analysts called it "one of the smartest strategies in business history." (It's interesting to note the difference between smart strategy and stupid strategy. If Bezos's plan hadn't worked, the same strategy wouldn't have been labeled as smart.)

Only a few years after Bezos launched Amazon.com, business analysts began questioning whether Amazon.com would ever see a profitable day. Many of these analysts were "out" on the investment and felt that Bezos was incapable of turning Amazon into a legitimate business. Many business strategists felt that Amazon .com should rein in its growth. Bezos, however, wanted to explode its growth—against the advice of experts. When the sound business advice suggests defining your niche, Bezos wanted the broadest consumer base—not considered smart strategy. It wasn't necessarily sound strategy that allowed Amazon to post amazing profits when other dot-coms evaporated; it was its leader's drive, imagination, and invention. Smart strategy is often left up to the results of a smart leader—an Anywhere Leader.

Entrepreneur Blake Mycoskie isn't necessarily a bad strategist. But he's not the poster child for brilliant strategy, either. He is a perfect example of a leader for progress who was sensitive to needs when he observed shoeless children in Argentina suffering from a debilitating and disfiguring disease called podoconiosis. Simply putting shoes on these children would protect them from the disease, which is caused by irritation from the compound silica in the soil. Moved by what he saw, Mycoskie launched a shoe company that donated one pair of shoes to a child in need with every customer purchase. That company, TOMS Shoes, is now a colossal success, identified by younger consumers as one of their favorite brands, according to a study by Outlaw Consulting.

Mycoskie perceived a need that he grew passionate for, and he got in front of a community of people around the world with a benevolent heart. There are many consumers who want to feel good about their purchase beyond pure self-indulgence. My wife has several pairs of TOMS Shoes, and she feels good about the part she's playing in helping fight disease every time she takes a step in her slip-ons. She's a member of the TOMS Shoes community. She's more than loyal to TOMS Shoes. She's an advocate. Mycoskie created more than a product. He enabled a community of givers, and he gave them an avenue to do good. He connected a product with a purpose—and built a growing company because of it.

Customers of TOMS Shoes are truly a *tribe*, to borrow a term from author Seth Godin—and Mycoskie found a way to lead it. "When you are doing something good," he once said, "people want to help you." In the case of TOMS Shoes, a lot of people. And that was always the goal. Mycoskie explained his philosophy in a 2009 *LAist* article: "It is not just being like we're a brand and we're doing it ourselves, but rather getting people to write about it, email about it, share the videos, write on the blog . . . it's really a very inclusive company so that we can get more people participating."

If you've seen the movie *Pirates of the Caribbean: The Curse of the Black Pearl*, you likely remember a scene in which Will Turner and Captain Jack Sparrow sneak out to commandeer a ship in the harbor. To reach the ship without being noticed, Turner and

Sparrow flip a small boat upside down and submerge it, walking across the ocean floor while keeping their heads in the hull of the boat where a little oxygen remains. "This is either madness or brilliance," says Turner, to which Sparrow replies: "It's remarkable how often those two traits coincide." The most imaginative plans are often madness—and those who often dare to pursue them are perceived as brilliant if things work out.

What some perceive as a maddening characteristic in leaders, others perceive as an incredible drive for progress—both daring and determined—a sensational curiosity for what's possible, and an amazing ability to be vastly resourceful with everything that is available. Put these traits together and madness becomes brilliant and leads to extraordinary work.

Amazon's Bezos was labeled irresponsible before he became brilliant with his drive, imagination, and invention. Mycoskie is celebrated because his brilliance comes from his heart, not just his mind. Both leaders dared to create a bold vision, and vision can be born from either madness or brilliance. The difference is in whether or not the leader behind the vision has the right motives, and whether or not she can produce the results through her drive for progress, her sensational curiosity for what's possible, and her resourcefulness. Walt Disney's plan for creating a large-scale family-oriented amusement park was madness before it became brilliant. Sam Walton was pounded by his retail peers who said a major discount store could never survive in a mid-market. Mr. Sam, as he's affectionately referred to by Walmart associates, just might be the biggest business success story in history. Anywhere Leaders turn madness into brilliance—dumb ideas into smart strategies.

———————

In Chapter One, I presented the traits of the Anywhere Leader: *driven for progress, sensationally curious,* and *vastly resourceful. Driven for progress* is why the Anywhere Leader operates with the right and proper motives and remains determined. Through their drive for progress, Anywhere Leaders give new initiatives, processes, or opportunities the right amount of thought; they take active and progressive steps to set up these initiatives well; and they are determined to see them through. They've done their homework and sought out the opinions and insights of experts and participants. *Sensationally curious* is why the Anywhere Leader is a consummate learner who continues to grow and improve herself, her team, and her work. *Vastly resourceful* is why the Anywhere Leader never gets stuck in uncertainty, but invents her way through setbacks and out of tough spots. When the answer book doesn't exist, the Anywhere Leader's resourcefulness helps her find or create new answers to new problems.

So far in this chapter, I've highlighted the significant value that Anywhere Leaders bring to their organization: progress and reconciliation by Mandela, invention by Bezos and Hughes, passion for good and right things by Mycoskie, and an ability to turn perceived madness into brilliance by all of them, including Disney and Walton. This value is realized because an Anywhere Leader's behavioral strengths bring significant advantages to their organization. The Anywhere Leader's behavioral strengths and associated traits are shown in Figure 2.1.

Now that I've provided Anywhere Leader examples and explained the value and benefit to the organization, let's look at the specific advantages these Anywhere Leaders offer over other leaders. Not surprisingly, the nine advantages stem from the Anywhere Leader's distinctive behavioral strengths.

Advantage #1: Anywhere Leaders Are More Discerning

Anywhere Leaders bring advantages to organizations because they are more *discerning* than other leaders. They make better decisions because they are more educated (not necessarily formally), more experienced (not necessarily tenured), and more aware than others.

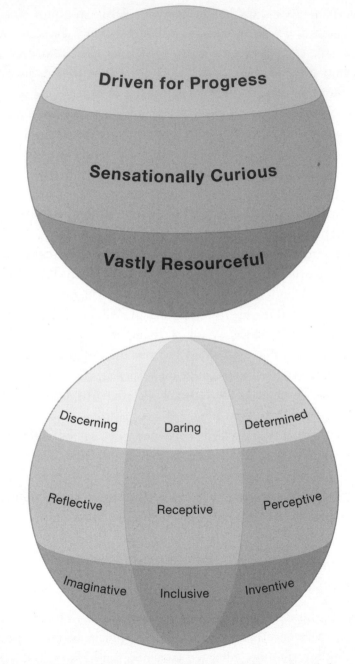

Figure 2.1 Three Core Traits and Behavioral Strengths of the
Anywhere Leader

Anywhere Leaders are lifelong learners who use any experience or encounter as a learning opportunity. Maybe that's why Anywhere Leaders have a difficult time journeying casually through life. These leaders stare at things longer, contemplate more possibilities, and have a hard time finding much of anything irrelevant. They are eyes-wide-open leaders. Their learning-for-discerning mindset enables them to make good decisions about how to proceed. The Anywhere Leader's judgment helps him determine what's worth fighting for and what should be avoided or left out. His experience and awareness helps him to identify the "watch outs" and anticipate barriers as he works through issues. Because of his discernment, the Anywhere Leader is rarely surprised or caught off guard.

Advantage #2: Anywhere Leaders Are More Daring

As initiatives progress, there should be no surprises, and even when there are, Anywhere Leaders are prepared to overcome them. They are *daring* leaders who willingly take on really big problems or pursue really big opportunities. When big challenges hit and others go into hiding, Anywhere Leaders have the courage to step in and step up. I have an incredible admiration for such people because they put themselves on the line when the stakes are high. Because they don't always play it safe, they are the pioneers of progress.

Jim Burke put himself on the line when the stakes were highest for Johnson & Johnson. Burke was the CEO of Johnson & Johnson when, in 1982, Tylenol capsules had been poisoned with cyanide, resulting in seven deaths in the Chicago area. Many experts thought that this would lead to the death of Tylenol, a product that held a 35-percent market share in the pain relief category. The thought was that no brand could withstand such consumer fear.

The problem was, Burke had no reference manual for dealing with this kind of crisis. He was going to have to jump into the ring and figure this one out for himself and for Johnson & Johnson.

Burke decided to meet the consumer fear head-on by being highly empathetic and highly visible to the public. He would make some significant commitments of company resources by pulling every Tylenol bottle off of every shelf (a very daring move), putting millions behind new security measures and new packaging for the product, and winning back consumer confidence through new promotions. Many thought that Burke was making a big mistake and encouraged him to lay low and let the public scare die down a little. The thinking was that too much visibility might be bad. But Burke remained steadfast. His daring moves and his determination helped Tylenol win back significant market share within just ten weeks.

Advantage #3: Anywhere Leaders Are More Determined

Anywhere Leaders are *determined* and not easily pressured away from a good and right idea—although they are open and flexible to various approaches and suggestions for carrying it out. Because they know how to prepare, they are often working on those strategic and transformational opportunities—the ones worth fighting for.

Today it seems more leaders give up on good ideas more quickly. In many organizations, good ideas last only until someone loses interest—strong starts, weak finishes. Organizational leaders are often easily excited by fads and shiny objects, but lose interest quickly when more effort than was first anticipated is required to meet expectations. This leads to organizational confusion. This pattern is even more apparent when it comes to digital strategies and initiatives. When a company unveils its digital strategy, many expect to see Zappos.com or Amazon.com results. When such results aren't achieved, the strategies are dumped and a shift is made. Anywhere Leaders aren't the ones behind this organizational ADHD. Sure, Anywhere Leaders are capable of shifting and adjusting, but they know a good plan when they see it. And they don't jump ship with the first setback, or the second, or even the third. Their determination helps ensure that a strong start delivers a strong finish as well.

Advantage #4: Anywhere Leaders Are More Reflective

An Anywhere Leader is *reflective*—thinking back on her experiences and capturing insights from her own mind. She internally processes what she observes and experiences, and from those observations she draws some internal conclusions. Because reflection is an internal process, the quality of being reflective enables her to make things personal as well—reflection on personal experiences helps her draw personal conclusions, making the target of an Anywhere Leader's curiosity . . . personal. The end result is a higher degree of commitment and a higher degree of engagement. I'm more engaged and committed to flying because I grew up around airplanes.

I'm still a Washington Redskins fan today—even though their performance has been inconsistent over the years—because I experienced Redskins games at RFK Stadium back in the glory days with Joe Theismann, John Riggins, and Art Monk. I'm committed to the Redskins despite their record because I reflect and connect to my experiences growing up as a fan. A large part of what keeps me engaged at SVI is my past experiences of our triumphs and our failures. Anywhere Leaders use their reflection to make a personal connection to the work and to the organization.

Advantage #5: Anywhere Leaders Are More Receptive

An Anywhere Leader is *receptive* to the ideas and conclusions of others. She takes what she has in her brain bank and adds the insights and experiences of others to capture more knowledge. I've come across these receptive leaders many times in my career, and they always impress me—not by how much they know, but by how much they ask. This tells me they aren't satisfied with their current knowledge; they want more. And more they get.

Try this experiment sometime—sit down and present a potential problem to a person who typically asks you a lot of questions before giving you any advice or insight. Then sit down and present the same challenge to a person who seems to always have quick and immediate answers. Then determine which meeting was the more informative and helpful. I'm willing to bet that the person who wanted to learn from you, who wanted your own insights before offering advice, provided more valuable and helpful information. That's a receptive leader—one who provides more valuable insight because she received more valuable knowledge and insights from others. These leaders provide more valuable insight because they are receptive to a broader base of inputs.

Advantage #6: Anywhere Leaders Are More Perceptive

Anywhere Leaders are more *perceptive* than others because they have a greater awareness and are more observant than others. They put their own experiences and what they learn from others to good use. Perceptive leaders aren't necessarily the ones who win the Trivial Pursuit games. They're not walking encyclopedias. Nor are they the Joe Fridays of the world who want "Just the facts, ma'am."

Perceptive leaders want the facts *and* the subtle undertones. Perceptive leaders want the actions *and* the motives behind the actions. They don't want some of the picture; they want the complete picture when it's available—and if it's not, their curiosity may drive them to try and complete the picture themselves. These leaders are sharp contemplators who can make sense of a lot of moving parts and missing pieces—and can put their knowledge, observations, and insights to work in the right direction. Perceptive leaders are aware of more ways to put more ideas into practice.

Advantage #7: Anywhere Leaders Are More Imaginative

There have been many articles over the past few years about the value that creative leaders bring. Our complex and challenging times call for people to—yes, I'll say it—get creative. Creativity requires imagination—our mind's eye, our visualization. Imagination allows the mind to wander, and to wonder a little more, about the "What ifs" and "Why nots" of our businesses. Imaginative leaders look around and see a relevant product for a new market, when others see an old and useless relic.

Have you ever seen the Pixar-produced film *WALL•E?* WALL•E was a robot left behind to pick up and compact Earth's trash, after every human had fled because Earth could no longer sustain life. No one was ever going back. But in all of the rubble and dust, the little robot saw some brilliant things and amassed an enormous collection of dazzling items. WALL•E ultimately inspired humans to return to Earth and restore their home.

Like WALL•E, imaginative Anywhere Leaders can often see in their mind's eye what others can't. And they are capable of dreaming up some creative ideas to meet business needs.

Advantage #8: Anywhere Leaders Are More Inclusive

Anywhere Leaders want to connect with other "imaginators." They want others in the room to introduce and discuss their ideas and to discuss the ideas of others. They want a bigger and better network of people to learn from and interact with. But these leaders don't just go glad-handing to expand their network. They're not interested in winning a popularity contest. What they are interested in is building strong and valuable relationships that they can use.

They are *inclusive* of many. Because they have strong and diverse relationships across their organizations, they can call upon and involve many to contribute. Their inclusive nature enables them to tap an abundance of talent throughout the company.

When a diverse many contribute to a business need, the advantages are abundant. Margaret Hart, in an article titled "Managing Diversity of Sustained Competitiveness," highlighted pharmaceutical giant DuPont Merck. The article presented the low sales of an anticoagulant drug in the Hispanic markets. When a Hispanic manager noticed that the drug was labeled only in English and recommended that DuPont Merck translate the instructions into Spanish for the Hispanic market, the company did—and sales improved significantly. Now, educational materials for the drug are translated into fifteen languages—and bring in millions of dollars in new business.

That's what Anywhere Leaders do—they draw on a diverse many to solve diverse problems and enable new opportunities for growth.

Inclusive leaders are enterprise thinkers. They have a deeper understanding of how to leverage a complex organization and all its parts—customers, suppliers, partners, and systems—in order to deliver important initiatives. A few years ago, business processes seemed more linear—an idea started with research and development (R&D) in a company's corporate headquarters. Operations executed the idea, marketing marketed it, and sales sold it. But with technology so accessible to everyone, helping to connect ideas, a traditional R&D organization can't keep pace with new products that are being developed in every corner of the world. Headquarters can no longer afford to be the only filter for all ideas. Gurus are in the field, too, and they need to be included. After all, they know the market needs better than anyone else at HQ.

I can't remember the last time I was in a meeting with just myself, SVI full-time employees, and our client. Nowadays, it's a rare meeting that doesn't include SVI partners, client partners, SVI contractors, client contractors, and other third-party suppliers. In fact, when we're brought in as a third party, we may include our own third parties—or should I call them fourth and fifth parties. Regardless, the ability to resource a broad base of talent, systems, and capabilities across an entire supply-chain system gives the inclusive, enterprise-minded Anywhere Leader incredible speed and scale advantages.

Advantage #9: Anywhere Leaders Are More Inventive

In addition to their inclusiveness, Anywhere Leaders are inventors who love to tinker with things. These leaders find unique solutions just by picking up items, flipping them around, turning them over, taking them apart, and putting them back together again. And these leaders are behind organizational growth and expansion. They find new fits, options, and opportunities, and new ways to put new inventions to work behind business needs. These *inventive* leaders help usher in new product offerings and identify new markets for expanding services and product lines. They are inventive because they have the ability to create or re-create something of value. These inventive leaders are behind brand rebirths such as those of Swatch watches and Vans shoes. The Volkswagen Beetle was practically dead before a pair of inventive minds— J Mays and Freeman Thomas—joined together to make it cool and relevant again to an entirely new audience of car owners.

Reinvention isn't limited to products. It can apply to people as well. Back when I was in high school, Bret Michaels was extremely popular as the lead singer for the rock band Poison. Twenty years later, the Bret Michaels brand is bigger than ever before, as he's been remarketed as a reality TV superstar.

Today's product lifecycle is much shorter than it used to be. Anywhere Leaders are tuned into new consumer demands. They, themselves, are new and improved producers and are behind brand rebirths, product inventions, and product repositioning. Coleman, a strong brand for campers, became relevant to adventurers when inventive leaders got involved; now kayakers and mountain bikers advocate the brand. Keep an eye out for Saab; this tired brand was once on the brink of collapse, but a few inventive leaders are tinkering away, and there seems to be momentum building.

Inventive leaders aren't only behind product inventions or repositions. They are also contemplating the new and improved organizational structure in hopes of capturing greater organizational efficiency and performance. Whatever the target, these inventive Anywhere Leaders are after the new and better way—helping to increase the value and success of their organizations in a finicky consumer–driven world.

Looking Ahead

Later chapters will give considerable time to helping you develop the behavior that ushers in Anywhere Leader advantages. Some of you may be thinking that although these behavioral advantages are valuable, your organization and culture just isn't set up to enable your development toward becoming an Anywhere Leader. You may be in an organizational culture that makes it very difficult to live out the traits and behaviors of an Anywhere Leader. But that shouldn't stop you. One of the most interesting things we found through our research is that the performance of an Anywhere Leader is not dependent upon her work environment. Anywhere Leaders have the ability to transcend bad cultures, disruptive employees, and unproductive or downright wrong strategies. They help their organizations recover from missteps. Their presence improves the business from the base that was established when they entered their role. They shepherd their organizations from desperate to stable, from stable to good, and from good to great. IBM needed its Gerstner to become stable, Apple needed its Jobs to become good, and the New Orleans Saints needed its Brees to become great.

Is there a more compelling recent story than the crowning of the New Orleans Saints as Super Bowl champions in 2010, and the heroism shown by Drew Brees? Brees exudes Anywhere Leader characteristics—but the New Orleans setting wasn't entirely conducive to his development as an Anywhere Leader. When visiting

New Orleans for the first time, Brees found himself unintentionally on the back roads, witnessing the significant devastation wrought by Hurricane Katrina. He connected with the devastation and began to reflect how New Orleans and he himself had both experienced tragedy, albeit on different scales—the population of New Orleans through Hurricane Katrina, and Brees as an individual coming off of a significant injury that many predicted would ruin his NFL career.

Brees started asking a lot of questions about how he could help New Orleans, rather than asking how New Orleans could help him. After accepting a contract to quarterback the Saints, he began making connections with others, inspiring hope and supporting recovery for the city. And he was determined on and off the field. Even though the Saints had lost their three final regular-season games, they persevered as champions in the end.

With his legacy secured, Brees is still significantly involved in recovery efforts in some of the most devastated areas in the city. The stories of Drew Brees, the New Orleans Saints, and Anywhere Leaders are *give* and *gain* stories. These leaders invest so much of themselves into the right and good things. Inevitably, they experience significant gain from their involvement—though the gain isn't their entire motivation.

That's why these leaders are transportable throughout your business. Put them on the good stuff or the bad stuff, and they will improve it. Put them in foreign territory and be confident that their impact will be felt in a most positive manner. I've seen Anywhere Leaders at work in even the harshest work environments. Their ability to remain and persevere as they drive change to improve the business is extraordinary.

So, do you want to be one of these Anywhere Leaders who is capable of being dropped into any setting and succeeding? Do you want to create more of these leaders in your organization? Then let's dive into the "how to" part of this book.

Part Two

DRIVEN FOR PROGRESS

3

MOTIVE DIFFERENTIATES THE ANYWHERE LEADER'S DRIVE

D riven for progress—what exactly does that mean? Not what it used to. A few years ago, progress was all about *you*—your advancement, your growth, your gain. It meant being the expert and making sure everyone knew it. But that doesn't fly today. In the new business world and for the Anywhere Leader, drive is different. To explain the difference, I'll have to start off with a little cognitive psychology talk. You might want to read this chapter while lying on a nice comfortable couch.

One of the most evasive and enduring questions in the field of psychology is "Why are some people more motivated than others?" Over the last several hundred years, psychologists have worked doggedly to explain why some of us are motivated and driven at times and others aren't. And although I admire their work, no single theory perfectly explains the motivating force behind an Anywhere Leader's drive. Some come close, such as Rusbult's investment theory, which says we're motivated by the things we've already invested ourselves in, or cognitive evaluation theory, which suggests that our drive comes from our need to be in control of our lives, or expectancy theory, which implies that motivation is a mixture of one's ability and one's expected rewards.

Our research shows that Anywhere Leaders are oriented for achievement, and they're confident in their ability to accomplish any challenge they take on. Maybe they even like the fact that they will be rewarded for their achievement. Who wouldn't? But Anywhere Leaders aren't driven to acquire money, or gain control, or see a return on investment for the time and effort they've put in. They're not motivated because things are moving forward; they're motivated to *make* things move forward in pursuit of the right goals. They don't just have drive; they have a *drive for progress*. Anywhere Leaders find progress in the work, not just the result—and that's a huge difference.

The drive theory that most closely aligns with the Anywhere Leader is McClelland's acquired needs theory. Sometimes called the learned needs theory, it suggests that our innate drives and subsequent motivation can change from one experience to another. This theory explains how our drive is targeted toward our basic need to achieve, to affiliate with others, and to reach a position of power. When we move to a new city and are driven to make new friends so we won't be alone, we are acting on the affiliation drive. However, after a few years in the community forming lots of friendships, our drive might shift to trying to accomplish something of value that we can be known for—the achievement drive. After a few years of one success after another, we may not be so driven to prove ourselves. Our drive might shift to securing a power position in the community.

How a leader captures power is where this theory doesn't mesh with the Anywhere Leader. I'm not saying that Anywhere Leaders don't pursue or embrace powerful positions—quite the contrary. They are often in power positions, and they have worked hard to get there. The difference is in the "how." Obtaining power sometimes means suppressing others—something the Anywhere Leader would never do, but that power players often do. Power players elevate themselves and their position to the detriment of others who may be challenging them.

Not the Anywhere Leader. Her vision goes far beyond personal power. She wants to ignite movements and create something bigger and better than herself. She wants to build tribes and communities behind valuable human endeavors. Sometimes Anywhere Leaders are highly visible and out in front, and sometimes they aren't. When other power players come in and attack their movement or tribe-building work, Anywhere Leaders may not counter, but they will most definitely grow more determined, working harder and faster. That's why people trust them and love them. Their motives are pure, right, and honorable, not self-indulgent.

So after all that psychology, here it comes—the Anywhere Leader theory of motivation: An Anywhere Leader's drive for progress comes from the need to discover and to find significance and meaning in the journey. It comes from the need to matter to others and to society—to notably contribute for the sake of humanity. This drive is found in a person when she sets out to do things that are bigger than she is and beyond her. Think of the writers of the Enlightenment—Adam Smith, C. S. Lewis, G. K. Chesterton, John Locke, and Jean-Jacques Rousseau—who wrote to create understanding beyond our world. Or the entrepreneurs who left steady, secure jobs to do something that, as Olympic gold medalist and snowboarder Shaun White once said, tingles their scar. If you're an Anywhere Leader, you're driven by goose bumps, not dollars or position.

Because they're not motivated by self-preservation, Anywhere Leaders are willing to challenge norms and defend unpopular positions for the good of the work. They've developed the poise to rise above conflict and maintain a sense of calm, knowing that if they focus on the project, all the drama and turmoil will simply fade away.

Driven for progress inherently means driven to succeed—but the Anywhere Leader doesn't measure success in dollar signs. Hefty bonuses and big promotions are nice, but they're the by-products of progress, not the end goals. Research supports the idea that money isn't everything—or even the main thing. A 1965 study by Harvard University shows that when people are personally motivated by pure accomplishment, the motivating power of financial rewards is weakened. Building on that research, the late Dr. David McClelland, a prominent psychologist, stated that achievement-oriented leaders see the value of money mostly as a measure of their success, instead of a reason to try harder. Doesn't that sound like an Anywhere Leader to you? There's no doubt that we look to financial rewards as a measure of our progress. When we are successful, our bonus confirms our success in our eyes and in the eyes of others. What easier way is there to judge your achievements than by having a quantifiable value attached to your work?

Because he prioritizes progress over personal gain, the Anywhere Leader is authentic. He looks for the right agenda, not necessarily his own self-serving agenda. Inspired by human endeavor, he's able to motivate others to reach past their safe zones to drive bold pursuits. In the 1920s, when British mountaineer George Mallory was asked why he wanted to climb Mt. Everest, he famously answered: "Because it's there." The Anywhere Leader shares that spirit. He takes the challenge because it's there, because it's right, and because the work is its own reward, and achieving results mean progress.

Some people might question whether drive is an innate trait, but in fact, there's no nature/nurture debate here. Research shows that anyone can develop a drive for progress. McClelland decided to put this idea to the test. As part of a multiday training workshop, he instructed a group of business professionals to *think, talk,* and *act* as if they all valued personal achievement over financial gain during the workshop. Two years later, he returned to find that the members of this group had been significantly more successful in achieving their career goals than coworkers who had received the same workshop training *minus* the emphasis on personal achievement. The more successful group of people simply adopted the right mindset to pave their way to greater success. It's no magic trick; you've got to think about getting better if you're going to do so. The majority of health care workers who work with cancer patients suggest that a positive attitude goes a long way toward fighting the disease. Some say that attitude is more important than the medication.

So if you've got the right mindset and positive outlook, then the only question is how to develop the drive of an Anywhere Leader under the right mindset. What is it that makes certain people drive for progress and strive for results beyond the proper mindset and attitude alone? David Shenk, best-selling author of *The Genius in All of Us*, once said that it's not like "some people are just genetically doomed to be lackluster and others are destined to be brilliant." Our experiences in life are far more significant in ushering our success than our genetic blueprint. How many stories have we heard about the hopeless rising up to achieve greatness? Have you seen the movie *The Pursuit of Happyness*? This was the true story of Chris Gardner, a homeless man who, through amazing perseverance and drive, became a self-made millionaire, successful entrepreneur, author, and motivational speaker. Gardner's genetics alone might have rendered him an angry alcoholic. But his exposure to an abusive stepfather fostered an intense drive in him to become something better—and nothing like his stepfather.

Another example is former defensive end Rudy Ruettiger. His genetics gave him dyslexia and a five-foot-six-inch stature. His upbringing encouraged him to be what all other Ruettigers are—Pennsylvania coal miners. But Rudy was a Notre Dame Fighting Irish fan with an intense love of football. And somehow, he defeated every preconceived notion that he should live the life of a miner, in order to pursue his "crazy" dream of playing for the Irish. Nothing else mattered but that single-minded pursuit of a different life—a better life—than the one he was "supposed to" live.

Drive and ambition are created by the misalignment of what everyone else expects you to be and what you expect of yourself—and the fear that they'll be right. That's the point where both the personal mission and significant resilience are born. Michael Jordan felt it when he didn't make the varsity basketball squad in high school. His coach didn't think he was ready. Jordan disagreed, and he worked extremely hard to prove his coach wrong. You might say that drive and ambition come from the negative voice of motivation: *I'll show them.*

Drive is so strong and so significant that at SVI a major part of our hiring decisions are made not from the resume, the GPA, or the acquired skills. Rather, we hire our extraordinary people by their stories. If you're at SVI, you've probably beaten cancer, lost a child, grown up in a toxic home environment, or experienced extreme poverty. In Warren Bennis and Robert Thomas's book, *Geeks and Geezers*, these experiences are described as "crucible experiences" or periods of intense heat. And it's during these trying periods that life's defining decisions are made and one's perspective grows. As does one's leadership.

One of my business partners, Autumn Manning, is an extraordinary leader with unbelievable ambition. In fact, there are few people who can match her level of drive and intensity. Over the past seven years of working together, I've often wondered how such ambition was developed in her. But hear her stories of the past, and you'll quickly get a glimpse. At age eleven, saddled with an abusive and alcoholic stepfather and a mom trying to fill the parental gaps while working two jobs, Autumn had to raise her three younger sisters. Now thirty, she has a hard time recalling the houses she had lived in, there were so many.

Early in her life, she dealt with challenges that many of us would have a hard time comprehending. She was used to hardship, and Autumn's hardships helped develop in her a personal resolve and determination.

So how do personal stories play into good leadership skills? Let's look at Tyson Foods as an example. SVI helped create, and now facilitates, much of Tyson's emerging leader program called LINC (Leaders Into Champions). This program has been labeled a best-in-class development program for high potential leaders. With LINC training, we focus not on developing skills, but rather on developing the right mindset. We want to establish the right attitude of Tyson's top leaders. What's different in our approach is that we ask these high-potential leaders to get really personal before they are accepted into the program. We ask them to be open and vulnerable. We want to know how they've been tested and how they overcame such significant trials and setbacks. The participants present their personal crucible stories to a team of executives in a fairly formal setting, and needless to say, it is a very intense, but valuable time. I'll never forget a comment made by one of the executives after listening to the stories of how his top talent overcame their personal struggles. He said, "I learned more today about leadership than in any of my previous years in the business world combined."

Looking back on my own life, I've had a number of what I call lightning strikes. First, there was our moving from town to town throughout my childhood, which forced me to get really comfortable with trying to make new friends. Some might say always being the "new" kid put me at a disadvantage. (It was a blessing in disguise, as it turned out, as I was forced to learn to make new friends, fast. If you ask me, disadvantage is totally underrated and undervalued.) As an Air Force brat, when I moved to a new town, I wasn't easily accepted by others—being the new kid and all. I did find my acceptance with a bunch of knuckleheads in middle school and junior high school. We got into a lot of trouble growing up, and because of it, my fate was seemingly sealed. "You're not going to amount to much, Mike." Boy, I heard that a lot. I started to believe it, too, as I celebrated C-level work as a rare departure from the D's and F's that I usually got. I was surrounded by stern, disapproving looks and "What are we going to do with this kid?" laments. Expectations of me were low, and after years of feeling the pressure to be something more without much success, I let it go. I arrived at a point where I had nothing to lose—and ended up gaining an incredible perspective.

I could embrace my inner ragamuffin.

Years later, my second lightning strike hit. My wife and I lost our first son, Blake, to leukemia. Although life hadn't been an easy bed of roses up until that point, fighting for Blake's life introduced a new level of agony, from pressure to sheer terror. I'm the dad, and my innate nature is to protect my child at whatever cost. I've never felt more helpless than when I could do nothing but watch— watch the doctors give everything they had to save my son—and fail. At that point, I realized how precious life is, and how I have absolutely no control over it.

I could embrace my insignificance.

There are significant advantages to feeling like an insignificant ragamuffin. You gain the proper perspective. You realize that no matter what, you're not that big a deal. You connect with your "grain of sand" nature. This is a good thing, because you lose a certain tendency to be overly self-protective. When you can let go of just a little of your self-absorbed, self-preserving nature, you can put yourself out there a little more. You're not using every ounce of energy to defend against humiliation, a lack of acceptance, or the consequences of failure. Your "right" perspective gives you the freedom to dream bolder and to dare bigger—to throw caution to the wind (the Wright Brothers did, literally). While your peers are stuck in a pressure state of self-protection, you're free to ignite movement because you're not in your own way.

But although one's personal story is the potential lightning strike to their drive and ambition, it's just one leg of a three-legged

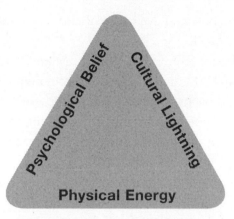

Figure 3.1 Three Components of an Anywhere Leader's Drive for Progress

stool (see Figure 3.1). There is science at work as well—though maybe to a lesser degree than the preceding examples can attest to.

Although basic temperament does not cast the die as to whether or not someone will be ambitious, a person who typically lacks energy will find it a little more difficult to develop a strong drive. Ambitious people are more persistent—exerting more energy to remain engaged, involved, and determined. The limbic part of our brain that is responsible for our emotions is the same part that is responsible for our drive. The brain takes in whatever it hears, sees, feels, smells, or tastes and decides whether or not to exert energy for an emotional reaction. Our drive works the same way. Our brain causes a reaction by releasing energy into our bloodstream, and we respond by either digging in or giving up. The more energy released, the more we dig in. The less energy released, the more we give up.

In many cases, our drive comes down to our belief. This relates back to the expectations we have of ourselves compared with the expectations others have of us. If we start to believe them and not ourselves, then we lose energy to move toward our goals or pursuits. We lose our persistence. But if we continue to believe in our capabilities, despite what others believe, our resilience and persistence remain—and even grow. Belief is a powerful force for the Anywhere Leader.

In 1954, Roger Bannister believed in himself and achieved a significant goal. He ran a mile in less than four minutes—something most people thought was physically impossible. Interestingly enough, within three years, sixteen other runners ran it even faster. One runner did it just fifty-six days after Bannister. The barrier to the four-minute mile wasn't physical at all. It was completely psychological. Once people started to believe such a feat was physically possible, others quickly followed.

Drive comes down to belief and the ability to overcome doubts and setbacks to become what you must become, also known as *self-actualization*. In 1943, psychologist Abraham Maslow presented a complex theory of human growth, which arranged people's needs into a hierarchy of priorities, with the need for self-actualization at the top. Things are much simpler in the animal world. All wolves aspire to be the alphas in the pack because—let's face it—the benefits are significant. Alphas have their bodily needs met before the betas: more food, more sex, and a strong likelihood of a long and healthy life. Humans also have an innate desire to survive; it's instinctive. But according to Maslow, our needs go well beyond food and water: they extend to safety, then love, then esteem, and, finally, to be everything we were meant to be. But like the wolves, many of us fall into beta mode. We're told we're betas, and we believe it. So we settle. We lose our drive and our ambition, and we accept the fact that we just might be eaten alive.

Drive is essential to becoming an Anywhere Leader. So how do you develop that trait if you don't already have it? First, ask yourself: *Are my expectations of myself aligned with everyone else's expectations of me? Have I been categorized as someone lacking energy and determination—a beta, not an alpha?* If you agree with your label, watch out. Complacency is about to step in if it hasn't already. Dare to elevate your expectations to exceed the expectations others have of you. Develop the courage to expect more from yourself.

Second, don't be blind to your experiences, glossing over them or trying to imagine them as less intense. Connect with them, no matter how painful they are. Use them to build stronger character and create your resolve. These experiences also help you keep other things in perspective—after all, you've survived the harshest of circumstances; surely a business challenge is a comparative cakewalk.

Describing the Anywhere Leader's drive is important because her assignments are usually tough, uncomfortable, unorganized, and ambiguous. Even when failure isn't an option, it's always looming. If you are an Anywhere Leader you can't lose your drive when things get tough or uncomfortable—or when you don't have a full understanding of the situation. You can't lose it when failure is waiting to pounce. Your drive must sustain you through it all. By developing a driven-for-progress mentality, you will be in the perfect position to capitalize on the leadership advantages of an Anywhere Leader.

An Anywhere Leader's drive for progress is magnified by the presence of the following three behaviors: *discerning*, *daring*, and *determined*. And it's important to develop all three to achieve the best results from your leadership.

A daring leader with no discernment suffers the most devastating consequences. Think about poor Charlie Brown. This highly compassionate, but often somewhat naïve character is a great example of someone who is quite determined, but not always the most discerning. No matter how many times his friend Lucy asks him to kick the football—only so she can pull the ball away at the last minute, sending him flipping through the air to land flat on his back—he falls for the same trick every time. Surely he should know better. But Charlie Brown's determination is too heavily weighted and not in proper balance with his discernment. He so wants to kick that ball, and he gets intensely focused on it. Why can't he just walk away? Doesn't he realize that Lucy is *always* going to pull the ball away at the last second? For Charlie Brown to become an Anywhere Leader, he has to temper his determination with discernment. Same goes for you—if you don't want to land flat on your back.

Many years ago, I was considering leaving a secure and lucrative job. I was an owner and president of an advertising agency and life was pretty well set for me and for my family. The money was good, but I was struggling with finding personal significance in my job. I had recently lost my son, and my business partner and I weren't always on the same page. I found myself evaluating how much effort I wanted to put into something that wasn't "tingling my scar." So I did what most of us do when we're up against such a significant decision; I sought advice from others I respected, and from books that looked interesting and relevant. I came across an interesting one called *Halftime*, by Bob Buford. This book helps people move from success to significance—how relevant! Although the book was full of value, there was one section in it that I couldn't disagree with more. Buford recommended having a plan B just in case a good plan A doesn't work out.

Ugh!

I don't ever want to live a plan B life. Plan B lives happen when determination fails. If I was going to leave my secure job, I wasn't going to easily settle for a plan B. That's when I started SVI—and it was twice as hard, twice as costly, and took twice as long to get up and running than I had originally anticipated. A discerning mind alone might have given up on this run. But discernment combined with determination kept me on the harder right path. Still does.

A daring leader without discernment can be categorized as narcissistic. He's the one making the big company bets based on ego. Sometimes his bold but thoughtless bets work out. But more often, they end up sinking him—and his company. Many people feel that John DeLorean's ego got in the way of any potential success of his car manufacturing company. DeLorean's car, named—

what else?—the DeLorean, was a seemingly promising sports car with a slick design, featured in the movie *Back to the Future*. The DeLorean ended up being punished and abused by a mad scientist who turned it into a time machine.

DeLorean, the man, lived an extremely lavish lifestyle, despite the fact that his company hardly ever got off the ground—it lasted only twenty-one months. He had the reputation of being vain, impulsive, and overbearing. His decisions were far from discerning, as he found himself wrapped up in a drug-smuggling scheme to generate cash for his company—though he was found not guilty, due to entrapment.

If only he had added a hefty dose of discernment to his sense of daring and determination, DeLorean might have had a shot at becoming a progress-driven Anywhere Leader—a very long shot. He would have also needed to acquire the other key traits: curiosity and resourcefulness. We'll cover those traits later in the book and examine the critical role they play in Anywhere Leadership. Without them, a drive for progress will likely go round in circles. But without drive—and the strengths of discernment, daring, and determination behind it—the other traits won't even get out of the gate.

Although much of this chapter has focused on having the right mindset, it's time to address behaviors that support an Anywhere Leader's drive for progress and how you can develop them. Let's start with the first behavioral strength under the driven-for-progress trait: discernment—the ability to determine the best course of action, or to tell the difference between right and wrong. In other words, discernment is having good judgment and making good decisions.

The question now is, how do you develop discernment?

4

BECOME DISCERNING

I'm amazed how little the quality of discernment is emphasized in a leader's development, and yet, with the exception of having right motives, it just might be the most critical quality of leadership. Good judgment enables you to make good calls—and considering how fast business moves today, you'll need to make a lot of them often, and quickly.

The average leader makes dozens of "leadership" decisions per day. By 2:00 P.M. each day, I've made roughly twenty-three—ranging from what my team needs to know in the weekly meeting, to how two managers should work through a conflict, to whether or not I need to be involved in a client meeting. What gives me the ability to make the right calls? How do I evaluate my decisions? How do I know if they are good, right, effective, or fair? In a word: discernment.

Discernment is everything. Passion without good judgment describes the Mel Gibsons of the world. These people have lots of opinions, but have no ability to rein them in so as to be most effective. Talk about unproductive: What about the person with an incredible work ethic but no ability to make good decisions? Like a hamster, he'll continue to spin the wheel for the sake of busyness, regardless of progress. His intellect lets him capture and understand every piece of data, but without discernment, he struggles to glean relevant and valuable insights from it. Likewise, the creative type who lacks discernment just might be the next Vincent van Gogh—tragically brilliant. She has a radical vision of how to change the way we think about click-and-mortar businesses, but cannot hold down a job long enough for anyone to take her seriously. Add good judgment to her mix of passion, work ethic, intellect, and creativity, and she becomes just plain brilliant.

I talked earlier about how personal experience fuels drive and ambition—but without discernment, past events and personal biases can lead to some pretty bad decisions. Past experience told the Head of Homeland Security that the levees in New Orleans would hold when Hurricane Katrina struck. Past experience told us that real estate investments were fairly secure. Past experience told communities in Detroit that their jobs were as secure as their fathers' jobs and their grandfathers' jobs. Can we rely on our experiences anymore? In a world with daily disruptions, rapid market fluctuations, and consumer access to an abundance of options, nothing seems to be lasting.

Without discernment, our experiences lead us to make assumptions that are often dead wrong. I made a bad assumption when I was teaching my daughter to ride her bike in our cul de sac. After I removed the training wheels and she rocketed down the street with ease, I assumed she could fully handle the bike, so I decided to introduce her to the world of "tricks on a bike."

"Alex, next time you pedal by me, slap me a high five with one hand."

"No, Dad."

"Alex, it's easy. Just carefully lift one hand and hang on to the handle with the other hand."

"No way, Dad."

"Alex, I promise, you'll be fine."

"OK, then."—Smack!

Do I need to say more? After the high five, she flew over the handlebars and onto the cement curb. Her forearm was bent at a 45-degree angle, with two bones broken. She was screaming, I was shocked and horrified, and my wife was ready to kill me. I had assumed that just because Alex could rocket down the street, she was ready for some tricks as well. Bad assumption.

The problem with assumptions is that they can catapult us too quickly to an idea that we can feel pretty comfortable and secure about. Our assumptions keep us from further discovery. They close off other relevant options. And if we're not careful, they can put us in a pretty myopic place. In his book *How We Decide*, author Jonah Lehrer explores what scientists refer to as the "sin of certainty," wherein our strong desire to believe we're right leads us to neglect evidence that we're *not* right. Just look at the subprime mortgage crisis. The investors working for "big, fancy hedge funds and big fancy investment companies" had all sorts of equations to measure risk, according to Lehrer. But they never questioned the underlying assumption that real estate prices wouldn't fall everywhere at the same time. "So they locked down on this belief . . . they were so certain that these things weren't risky."

We've all been there at some point—the place where we boldly commit ourselves to a direction feeling overconfident, only to be blindsided by unpredicted scenarios. Anywhere Leaders aren't myopic. Even when they move confidently forward with an idea based on solid research and personal knowledge, they are always a little cautious and alert, looking out for the unexpected. These leaders balance their confidence with a healthy amount of suspicion. Balance is the key here. We're all familiar with leaders who are overly suspicious and therefore stifled. Their unchecked paranoia keeps them from progress, and they fall into a continuous loop of maintaining the status quo—missing out on timely opportunities.

Being a discerning leader isn't about making a good decision, but rather about forming the habit of making good decision after good decision. To become a discerning leader, you need to immerse yourself in a constant state of evaluation. It means continuously gathering and analyzing information, seeking various points of view, and scanning the horizon for coming shifts. Because these leaders never view their decisions as static, they aren't consumed by trying to make the perfect call. They can confidently move forward, knowing that they can, and will, make adjustments as they go.

Nestlé, like many other consumer packaged goods (CPG) companies, has thousands of products in the marketplace, from hot cocoa mix to Willy Wonka candies. They have worldwide distribution and get their products into some extremely remote markets. To be operationally efficient, Nestlé must operate within certain product standards—size, shape, price point, and quantity. But local markets and retailers can be fairly demanding on Nestlé and other CPG companies, requesting special stock-keeping units (SKUs) that can be available and sold only at a particular retailer. Sam's Club may request an eight-ounce box of candy when the standard size is six ounces. That request from Sam's Club forces Nestlé to customize their product in order to meet it. Retailers often make such requests, and Nestlé must be able to quickly determine the size of the prize for such customization. Because there are significant special needs for large retailers, Nestlé and other CPG companies set up entire local market teams to meet specific retailer and market requests. They do this because they need discerning leaders on the ground making good and speedy decisions for when to distribute the standard product SKUs in a retailer and when to customize for new market opportunities.

For today's discerning leader, the decision isn't about a mindless charge forward. It's about continuous evaluation of the right opportunities. At Nestlé, managers reject the false choice of "standardize or bust." They determine—as professionals—when standardization makes sense for the worldwide market, and then quickly assess how to customize to meet the needs of an important local market.

Consider Toyota, the quality champion of the automobile industry just a few years ago. Toyota committed so thoroughly for so long to continuous improvement that the organization was the subject of dozens of books and case studies. Now they are a case study for different reasons, as observers and competitors analyze how Toyota's legendary culture resulted in sticking brake mechanisms and other product and service failures. An article in the February 2010 issue of *Fortune* magazine, titled "How Toyota Lost Its Way," states that "In the past, Toyota's strong operational skills obscured the need for any change in this structure." Allow me to paraphrase: Toyota's past operational excellence and experience ushered in an unhealthy level of arrogance.

In the article, one high-ranking Japanese executive said he detected an attitude at Toyota that "What we have been doing is right, and therefore we seem to know the world better." But it seems that the world knows better. The business world is calling for faster responses to consumers, more leverage across the organizational enterprise (field offices and suppliers), and widespread change in attitude and approach. Not Toyota. Toyota isn't doing much to increase its response time to its customer; it continues to maintain significant control at its Japanese headquarters; and it doesn't seem to be considering some recommended adjustments from field and regional offices. Instead, the company is reemphasizing the fundamentals that are now questioned by so many. You can't help but question the discernment of Toyota's leaders when they are failing to adjust to today's savvy consumer expectations. Clearly, The Toyota Way of the past needs a massive tune-up. At the very least, Toyota leaders could shift from arrogance to openly evaluating, analyzing, and listening—not only to their business, but also to their markets.

To be a discerning leader, you need to consider past experiences and assumptions, while being careful not to bank on them. You have to validate your assumptions by looking for, listening to, and analyzing all available information. And you must remember that the decision-making process is never complete; rather, it is continuously evaluated. Why? Because there are no predictable pathways that you can completely rely upon. As soon as an approach seems reliable, something shifts that directly or indirectly impacts our most strong and sturdy plans. Anywhere Leaders don't try to identify old patterns to solve new problems; they manage the paradox, making timely adjustments. And they effectively navigate through the unknown because they are constantly evaluating.

There are hundreds, maybe thousands, of books about discernment—having good judgment so that you can make good decisions and the right choices. But they don't explain the role of discernment in Anywhere Leadership. The Anywhere Leader's evaluation of a good choice can't be baseless or up for debate. Her good judgment leading to good choices must be based on the drive for progress, not on maintaining stability—based on the betterment of the team, not on self-promotion. Her choices must be more about significance and meaning than personal comfort—more about discovery than the status quo. What about you . . . what do you base your judgment on? When you make choices, is your priority to protect and promote yourself? Do you judge situations according to how they affect you personally, rather than how they affect your team or the work? What is the first thing you think of when your situation suddenly changes—the impact it will have on you or the impact it will have on your project?

The point is that to be an Anywhere Leader, you must have a higher standard of discernment than the average Joe or Josephina. You must make decisions in favor of progress—no matter how disruptive, unclear, or challenging your circumstances are. And you have to be ready and able to readjust your thinking as those circumstances shift. It's not easy. Reaching that higher standard of discernment requires that you effectively manage the paradox between your consistency and your willingness to change. Sound a little difficult? The rest of this chapter will provide recommendations for how you can be that discerning leader who is capable of making good decisions when things aren't certain and the answers aren't always clear.

Recommendation #1: Have Uncompromising Values and Compromising Behaviors

It's fairly obvious that in these times you must be an alert and adaptable leader ready to take on new priorities and business shifts. You've got to be able to drive change in your organization, lead through ambiguous and uncertain circumstances, and embrace newly rolled-out initiatives that you may be unfamiliar with. With continuous disruptions to your business, you can't be so set in your ways that you are too narrow-minded, and therefore easily blind-sided by a sudden or surprising turn of events. To keep unexpected changes from knocking us to our knees, we've got to remain nimble. But don't we also depend on consistent leaders who operate based on a strong set of values? We trust these leaders because we know how they are going to process and react to things. Therein lies the paradox—when to be consistent and firm in your position, and when to be open to change and adjust your behavior.

A discerning leader manages this paradox well. Why? Because he is both consistent in his values and ideals, and open to change in his behavior. Consider this illustration: A sailboat is a fairly nimble vessel. Its sails serve as wings that use wind to push the boat through the water. By adjusting these sails, you can turn the boat very quickly and aggressively. Up on the deck are many ropes called lines, which move any number of sails to help effectively maneuver the boat. It's pretty interesting to stand at the helm and see so many parts and rigging dedicated to making quick adjustments. You need all those parts, because wind never stays consistent. To captain a sailboat, you must always be evaluating the conditions and making the adjustments. You have to be ready to adjust to changes at any time. If you aren't ready and able to do so, you'll quickly find yourself off course, and you won't make it to your destination.

There's another essential part of a sailboat called the keel—a strong structural element found underneath the hull of the boat. The keel extends deep into the water to hold the sailboat upright and keep it from flipping over from the wind pushing against the sails. The keel counterbalances the force of the wind on the sails. It serves as the foundation of the boat and is its strongest structure. The bigger the boat, the bigger the keel.

Discerning leaders who are both consistent and adaptable are like that sailboat. On the surface they're adaptable and nimble, able to leverage the wind and adjust to changing conditions. Underneath they're steady and firm. (See Figure 4.1.) The Anywhere Leader has a strong personal keel that keeps him steady.

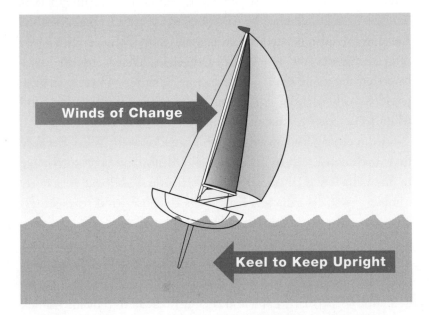

Winds of Change

Keel to Keep Upright

Figure 4.1 A Discerning Leader Manages Stability with Agility

It represents his deeply rooted core values and principles, which hold him upright when the strong winds come. The Anywhere Leader also has a lot of rigging—a broad base of skills and talents, and accessible resources and relationships that keep him nimble, able to make quick and necessary shifts and adjustments based on changing conditions. He knows how to use a lot of options to set the proper course—and he likes making adjustments because they help make him a much better performer.

Wal-Mart founder Sam Walton adjusted to the winds of change by opening new markets, changing his inventory, and embracing new ideas for low-cost efficiencies. But he held fast to three core values that he never changed (his keel)—having respect for individuals, always striving for excellence, and serving the customer. A tornado couldn't shake loose those values. Anywhere Leaders need to determine their core values, their principles—those things that nothing can sway. Think about your leadership: Do you have an immovable set of values? It's important to know yourself, to know what you stand for personally and professionally, so that when mega-change comes, you stay upright. When you behave in a way that contradicts your core values, you put yourself in danger of getting sunk. Having a set of principles makes decision making easier; if you're pressed to do something that counters them, you won't do it. Once you confirm those immovable values, however, everything else is up for discussion, debate, and change.

Your core values come from your beliefs. After all, you behave in a way that supports your beliefs. If I believe the statement "What goes around, comes around," then I'm going to treat others as I want to be treated. If I believe that people are the most important asset of any company, then I'm going to prioritize their needs. Your beliefs may come from science, experience, or faith. Science has proven this thing called gravity; therefore, I won't go skydiving without a parachute. Experience taught me as a kid that a hot stove will burn you; therefore, I won't touch it. My faith tells me to love my neighbor; therefore, I will strive to be benevolent to others in need. Core beliefs are just that: what is essential and fundamental for your good and productive life. Ideally you should have no more than five core beliefs. What three to five core beliefs are essential to your good and productive life?

There are many examples of leaders who went too far with their core values, using them for destruction and then hiding behind them to avoid personal accountability. Their leadership keel was way too big for their boat. One example is Al Dunlap, CEO of Sunbeam from 1996 to 1998. He had a core belief in profits at any price, and his behavior supported it. Dunlap became known as Chainsaw Al for his hatchet jobs on corporate workforces. Chainsaw Al was blind to other options and insensitive to culture.

At the time, some defended his close-minded decision to drive shareholder value at the expense of everything else. But what ultimately proved impossible to defend was how he lost all ethical integrity in trying to grow shareholder value at Sunbeam—pushing the ethical and legal limits of generally accepted accounting principles—a move that put him on the wrong end of class-action lawsuits for fraud brought about by, interestingly enough, Sunbeam shareholders. Pursuing profits is a legitimate core value, but doing it "at any price" is where Dunlap became blind, ignorant, and destructive.

What about you—are you leaving a trail of destruction in your wake? As you consider the things you can be open to adjusting in order to be a more effective leader, what comes to mind? Where are you too rigid in your approach and too myopic in your thinking? Where do you need to make some changes in your behavior? Have you had various other people approach you multiple times about a similar issue—your own blind spot that others see?

Anywhere Leaders, though firm in their beliefs and values, are typically moveable and willing to adjust their own leadership modus operandi (method of operation, or M.O.).

You do have one, you know. All leaders have an M.O. that defines their approach to managing and decision making. Anywhere

Leaders are moveable, and they're willing to adjust their M.O. to match any set of circumstances. If they weren't, their typical approach might get in the way of a good decision. For example, I don't really want a highly collaborative fire chief gathering all of his staff around, discussing how to save my child from our burning house—that's a poor decision under those circumstances. I want that fire chief to take immediate action and bark out commands. That situation calls for more of a command-and-control leadership behavior. In business, however, a command-and-control leader can squash innovation—a collaborative process that requires creative thinking, research, debate, and a lot of tinkering. A control-driven leader makes poor choices and poor decisions when collaboration is needed. A collaborative leader makes poor choices and poor decisions when critical and decisive action is needed fast. Whether your M.O. is collaborative or closer to command-and-control, you may need to adjust it to effectively address the situation.

A discerning leader knows when to adjust and when to remain firm. Are you able to adjust your behavior to meet new situations without compromising your principles?

Recommendation #2: Choose the Greater Good

Anywhere Leaders make careful decisions based on the success of the collective group—which is why Dennis Kozlowski, former CEO of Tyco, isn't an Anywhere Leader. Under Kozlowski's reign, Tyco thrived. This should have been a great story of a great leader who did great things. But Kozlowski is currently serving time in a New York prison for receiving unauthorized compensation. Kozlowski got greedy, having Tyco fund a significant amount of his luxury houses and his lavish lifestyle, including one hellacious party for his wife on her fortieth birthday. But Kozlowski is just one name on a long list of some pretty greedy leaders—Kenneth Lay of Enron, John Rigas of Adelphia, Bernard Ebbers of WorldCom, and too many others to list.

Now compare those guys with Blake Mycoskie, the social entre-preneur and founder of TOM's Shoes whom I introduced earlier. Mycoskie is one of a number of Gen-Y (or Millennial) leaders who have focused their business on social awareness and social action. These young leaders are caught up not in themselves, but rather, in the collective—this is a hallmark of their generation. And their genuine love and concern for others is appealing to so many who follow them.

When Anywhere Leaders of any generation are given two options—one that significantly elevates them and suppresses others, the other one that benefits all—the decision is easy: drinks all around. These leaders are the first to lend a hand or go beyond their own job definition to help someone else. They don't ask more of their team than they do of themselves, and they don't lead from behind the desk. Anywhere Leaders are out in front; they roll up their sleeves and get dirty alongside everyone else. Being with the collective doesn't just allow them to build loyalty; it puts them in a better position to make good calls for the business and for the team. It gives them empathy—a priceless commodity, particularly in difficult times like these.

The tough economy of 2008 and beyond has hit practically every company in one way or another. Like so many organizations, one hospital system that SVI supports, Washington Regional Medical System, had to make significant budget cuts a while back. I remember how the CEO sent a letter to his leaders asking them to think about forgoing their expected bonus and annual pay increase in order to spread the money throughout the workforce and avoid layoffs. Every one of those leaders chose the collective over themselves, and it sent a powerful message to the entire orga-nization. The following year, Washington Regional set new records for patient satisfaction and employee engagement.

How are you processing your decisions? As you make choices, don't just consider the collective—act for the sake of the collective. Those are the better decisions, and you will benefit in the long run.

Recommendation #3: Embrace a Healthy Dose of Suspicion

I'm sure there are "get rich quick" success stories out there, but I have yet to see one. The stories that I've heard are the ones that start with lots of promise and passion for easy money but end with significant losses and career restarts. I find it funny how these easy-money guys are always trying to get other people involved. My question is, why *not* hoard the riches? Oh, maybe they're serving the collective! Hardly. In the end there's always some reason their scheme just didn't work out—it took too long, or someone was wronged along the way . . . whatever. We need to have a healthy dose of suspicion with these encounters.

On the opposite side of the spectrum from the easy money entrepreneur we find the permanently passive manager. This manager has an unhealthy level of fear and insecurity. If the easy money entrepreneur is overconfident, this manager is overcautious. He is downright afraid of screwing something up, so he makes decisions to protect the status quo at all costs.

The Anywhere Leader fits right between these two extremes. Her desire for progress pushes her to defend against a tendency to be overcautious. Anywhere Leaders are somewhat wary, but their suspicion drives their curiosity, as opposed to shutting down their interest altogether. Their healthy level of caution pushes them to dig a little deeper, and not race blindly into a perceived great opportunity. Anywhere Leaders find the healthy ground between over cautious and overconfident behaviors—and because of it, their decisions are timely and well thought out. That's where you need to be, too.

Are you a discerning leader? Keep these points in mind as you strive to make good and effective choices (discernment) as an Anywhere Leader.

1. Make decisions that don't compromise your core values.

2. Adjust your leadership behaviors to make good decisions for a given situation.

3. Make decisions in favor of the collective group.

4. Approach your decisions by being neither overcautious nor overconfident for progressive and effective growth.

5

BECOME DARING

I'm not much of a gambler, but I've been to Vegas a few times, and I've watched countless people sit at a roulette table for hours with a big pile of chips. Sometimes they hit it big and sometimes they lose big. Some people walk away and cut their losses, but what about those others? What about the people who just don't have that ability to get up and leave when the chips are down? Those people play recklessly, betting it all on luck, time and time and time again. They demonstrate addictive behaviors, seeking instant gratification over smart moves—why? Because they succumb to the gratification of short-term pleasure, rather than using the discipline required for longer-term success.

I don't know about you, but I don't want reckless people leading my business. I do want people with some guts, however. To drive progress is to move things forward. And it takes some guts to move things forward beyond the status quo. By nature, people who are driven by a vision of progress dislike the status quo. These people are motivated to advance when they think there's a better way, a better idea, or a better opportunity. These progress leaders are passionate about potential and committed to seeing it through. Is there a story of great progress and advancement where a highly risk-averse person was at the helm? Not likely.

One of my heroes is Liz Murray, whose story was told in the Lifetime movie *Homeless to Harvard.* As a young teenager, Liz lost both of her parents to AIDS. She had nowhere to go, so she ended up on the street with a bunch of other homeless kids. At this point, Liz could have given up and accepted life as it was set up for her—homeless, possibly contracting AIDS herself, and who knows what else. But Liz expected more, and she took a chance. While homeless, she applied to Harvard. That in itself is an amazing accomplishment and a very daring and bold move. But her boldness paid off: she was accepted. The rest is history. Liz is one of the most sought-after speakers around the world, a best-selling author and a successful entrepreneur. When others accepted their circumstances and gave up, Liz had the courage to pursue her dreams.

Not all bets or bold moves work out so well. We're familiar with those stories, too. The young actress gives up college to move to LA and become a movie star, only to end up becoming a late-night bartender. The corporate manager gives up a somewhat secure job to start his own dude ranch—ultimately finding lots of time to work on his resume for the next somewhat secure job. The struggling musician performs his heart out in the hotel lobby only to be told to shut up so people can hear the game on TV. But thank God for those who dare, because for every ten thousand who fail, there are two or three who end up giving society a better way.

Elizabeth Hurley, that struggling actress who tended bar in the 1980s, is now a fashion icon and a savvy business owner. Tim Westergren was the struggling hotel lobby musician who was asked by that sports fan to stop playing so he could hear the latest football scores. That lightning strike gave Tim what he needed to start one of the most successful online businesses—Pandora. Sure, these leaders are smart, but it's important to remember that they started out in very humble states. Their success began with courage. When others wouldn't, they did.

What about the other 9,998 people who dared to dare? It's easy to highlight the successes, but aren't there many more stories of disappointment and failure? Sure. But few of those people actually died trying. Their bold moves didn't usher in complete hopelessness for a lifetime. After all, Hurley dared and failed. So did Westergren. So did Walt Disney. Failure, setbacks, and crucible moments are often the fuel behind the most courageous leaders we know. My ability to take on a few risks, whether I failed or succeeded, continues to be a force that pushes me to drive progress and achieve some pretty valuable milestones. I'm not the most courageous person, but I embrace my need for taking on a few adventures. When others won't, I often will. My willingness to dare to do comes from a few of my own lightning strikes, my beliefs, and a whole lot of persistence.

But I'm with you. I'm sure there are those out there who dare to do, and still go through life without ever catching a break. It's not just bad luck, however. Sometimes, many of them lack a key element—determination.

Without determination, a daring move gets the best of you every time. Daring moves are higher-risk bets. Rarely is one swing of the bat going to pay off. The courageous ones swing and swing and swing until they make contact. The Wright Brothers dared to fly. Let's face it; flying in the early 1900s took a lot of courage. After all, people were making lots of attempts and even managing to get airborne, only to lose control and fall fatally to the ground. And although Wilbur and Orville experienced their share of nasty crashes, they remained determined. After hundreds of attempts and just as many failures, on December 17, 1903, at Kitty Hawk, the first controlled and powered aircraft, the Wright Flyer 1, took off, flew eight hundred feet, and landed successfully.

Anywhere Leaders know that their daring moves don't stand a chance without a high degree of commitment, perseverance, and personal resilience. Like the Wright Brothers, Elizabeth Hurley, Liz Murray, and Tim Westergren, these leaders don't believe in the easy money "get rich quick" schemes. They realize that worthy pursuits are rarely easy, but they're always worth the sacrifice.

So who are the opposites of the Anywhere Leader? They are the self-absorbed, safe players who give up easily. They are the ushers of the status quo—not the drivers of progress. In today's business environment, you don't want to be one of these ushers, because their toxic combination keeps them grounded in mediocrity, with a business-as-usual mindset in a rapidly progressive world.

In my observation, the best leaders are those who push close to the edge without going over it. We glamorize these "risk takers," painting them as larger than life. What's interesting is that these leaders, though courageous, aren't necessarily comfortable in positions of risk. They may push to the edge, but they probably have a few sweat beads on their foreheads when they do. They're not larger than life. They are as concerned with their safety and with their security as anyone else would be. They weren't born with some *daring* chromosome that made them fearless. But despite some element of discomfort, nervousness—even fear—they are compelled to act in daring ways for the sake of progress. They've developed the fortitude to make tough, even risky, calls when things just aren't certain.

Recommendation #1: Playing It Safe Isn't Safe—or Smart

At almost every company I've worked with, top management has expressed the desire for leaders who have the courage to take some well-calculated risks. But it's interesting how careful they are with their wording. They don't want dumb risk—they want *smart risk*.

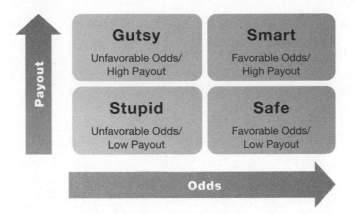

Figure 5.1 Smart Bets Grid

What does that mean, exactly? Better odds? Small gambles instead of big ones? Or do they want people taking on only those risks that are sure to pay out? (What's risky about that?) The top brass may encourage a daring nature in their leaders, but often with a proverbial wink, wink: "I want you to take more risks with our business, just don't screw it up." Talk about mixed messages.

The Anywhere Leader knows that in order to succeed, her daring moves must succeed. That's why she doesn't make bets of pure chance. The Anywhere Leader doesn't cross her fingers just hoping that the luck of the draw is in her favor. Instead, she determines the odds, and makes bold moves that have achievable outcomes. Look at the Smart Bets Grid in Figure 5.1. Which of the categories do you think she falls into?

By analyzing the odds and considering the potential, the Anywhere Leader takes smart risks. She never gambles when the odds are significantly unfavorable and the gains are insignificant. Nor will she take favorable odds that are somewhat meaningless in value. After all, she wants progress, growth, and advantage— not the status quo. Where do you fall on the Smart Bets Grid? Are you calculating both the odds and the payoff? Do you find yourself playing it safe, or are you being overly gutsy? Consider your decisions about risk, and strive for the upper right-hand corner of the grid. These daring moves don't just change the game; they tip it in your favor.

Recommendation #2: Choosing Challenge over Chance

So you want to be smart. Great! But don't stop there. Lots of people are smart—but they still fail under certain conditions. Anywhere Leaders don't just want to be smart; they want their bold moves to set themselves, their teams, and their companies apart from others. They're looking for a payoff that will help them effectively navigate and lead through uncertainty. How do Anywhere Leaders turn a "smart" daring move into a "set apart" daring move? Simple. They calculate the odds—and then figure out how to swing them more in their favor.

Being an entrepreneur, I've often been reminded, especially by banks, that most businesses fail within the first three years. It's true; the odds of success aren't good. But building a business isn't a game of chance. Successful entrepreneurs work really hard and really smart—and their effort and intellect help swing the odds more in their favor.

Here's an example. Debbie, an Anywhere Leader, transfers to the Dublin office to lead a team that's been struggling with turnover and lagging in performance. The Dublin office is responsible for the company's online retail presence—the primary growth engine for the entire organization. The company needs to grow its online sales by at least 50 percent each year. Obviously, for the overall success of the company, the success of the Dublin office is essential. The stakes are high—but so is the potential.

Debbie is the third leader to take over this group in the last four years. Based on that alone, you might think she's got, at best, a 30-percent chance of success. But Debbie has been in this position before with a similar situation. Once she was assigned to turn around the Pittsburgh office, and within a couple of years Pittsburgh was setting performance records for the company. Debbie feels that her experience, effort, and intellect will swing those odds of success from 30 percent to 70 percent. She sees some similarities between Dublin and Pittsburgh, and she's confident she can make it work. Although 70-percent odds are no guarantee of success, she's willing to take the job, because it could push her into the executive ranks, establish a competitive advantage for the company she loves, and give the one hundred people in the Dublin office a new sense of hope.

Let's revisit the Smart Bets Grid again. Except this time I've added an element for effort and intellect (see Figure 5.2).

The application of effort and intellect should help improve your odds and increase your payoff. It lets you move from a "smart" risk to a risk that "sets you apart" from others. As you assess your courageous and bold moves, consider the upper right-hand quadrant labeled "Smart." But also consider your experience, your effort, and your intellect. Do they help you shift the odds more in your favor, or is your move completely dependent on chance? When others have unfavorable odds and are hesitant to make an

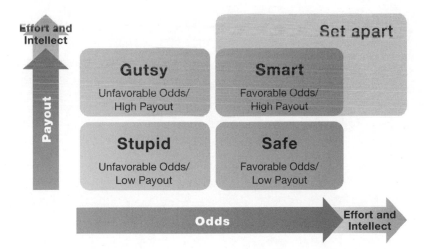

Figure 5.2 Set Apart Bets Grid

attempt, are you able to swing the odds your way, make the attempt, and establish a significant competitive advantage?

Anywhere Leaders place bets on their efforts and their intellect. They neither play it safe nor leave their risks purely to chance. What about you? If you're making daring and bold moves that are left purely to chance, stop. Make sure the odds of your big-bet risks can be improved by your effort and intellect.

6

BECOME DETERMINED

*Oh God . . . Encourage us in our endeavor to live
above the common level of life. Make us to choose the
harder right instead of the easier wrong, and never to
be content with a half truth when the whole can be
won. Endow us with courage that is born of loyalty to
all that is noble and worthy, that scorns to compromise
with vice and injustice and knows no fear when truth
and right are in jeopardy. Guard us against flippancy
and irreverence in the sacred things of life. . . .*
— *The Cadet Prayer, West Point*

I love this prayer (a portion of which is presented here) and what
it represents. The cadets are asking for the strength not to be
motivated by what's easy and comfortable. They want to pursue
the honorable and the significant things of life, even when it's
difficult to do. Like the Anywhere Leader, they are driven for

progress in pursuit of the uncommon life for themselves and for others.

Some might call the ideals expressed in the Cadet Prayer a naïve pursuit by a bunch of kids who've never really been tested. It's all well and good to recite these words in a classroom, and the feeling may be genuine, but what about when things get intense? Well, that's the whole point. The Cadet Prayer is an acknowledgment of weakness. It is a plea for discernment to choose the harder right over the easier wrong—and for the determination to stick with it.

That's what determination is: the ability to pursue the right agenda to the end, even if it's difficult and costs you something in the process. To be an Anywhere Leader, you must be willing to take steps to address a problem or a challenge, even if it's not the easiest solution for you. Going for ease won't address the true nature of the problem. Even if the right move ends up being the hardest move, it's still right—and you still have to make it in order to meet the goal.

Think of D-Day and Omaha Beach. Every step of that long-planned invasion was a disaster. Rough seas swallowed up ten U.S. landing crafts before they even reached the beach. Bad weather delayed the landing of other vessels, and navigational difficulties kept most of them from hitting their target. The Germans launched an unexpectedly fierce defense. More than two thousand U.S. troops died trying to take that beach. The survivors could have surrendered, but they didn't—and ultimately they prevailed. They knew their mission was critical, and despite their heavy losses, they would not abandon it.

The heroism of those troops is significantly incomparable to our business challenges, but the story of Omaha Beach illustrates the very meaning of determination: moving forward under difficult circumstances, through and around obstacles, despite setbacks and potential losses. That's what the cadets are talking about and praying for. Pursuing the harder right demands more resilience, more effort, more determination—and Anywhere Leaders have all three. They have a greater resolve to remain committed and not quit. Their ability to stay in the game even when they are behind allows them to pull off some heroics in the end. So how can one develop determination and resolve?

Recommendation #1: Grow Your Zone of Objectivity

Everyone likes to feel powerful, particularly against forces that threaten their ability to succeed. But increasing your power can actually decrease your objectivity—a key weapon for overcoming obstacles and making good choices. When you focus on power and gain it, you can become overconfident, even arrogant. But just as power can skew your ability to make good decisions, so can fear and caution brought about by a loss of power. Yes, I presented this caution/confidence equation in the discernment segment, but hang in there with me—it is central to determination as well. Look at the model in Figure 6.1.

All of us have a Zone of Objectivity. It lies squarely between our desire for power and our sense of fear. That's the place to be. Without keeping my power in check, I will lose objectivity. I'll develop more and more false confidence until I become arrogant and stupid—and then I will inevitably do something completely irresponsible. (That's why we have laws to try and keep powerful people accountable.) When I become irresponsible and make some huge mistake that brings tough consequences, I'll lose all my confidence—and crash. And once I crash, my commitment and determination will crumble. It sounds a bit doomsday-ish, I know. But that's what often happens to leaders who lack objectivity. We already know what happens to leaders who cannot manage their fears: absolutely nothing. They find it difficult to create any meaningful record of accomplishment because they've taken themselves out of the action.

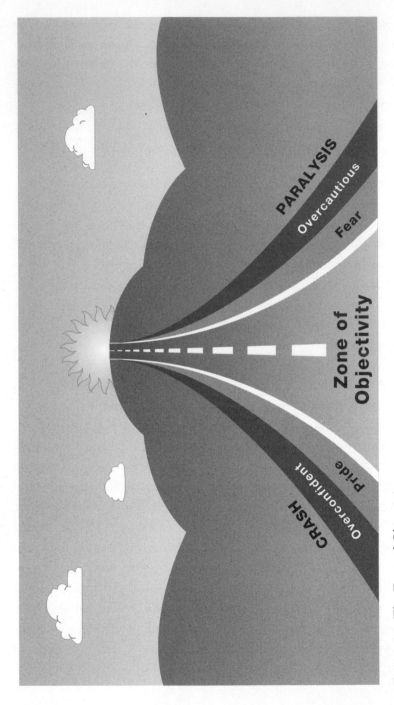

Figure 6.1 The Zone of Objectivity

I recall the story of two senior executives at a Fortune 500 company who were competing for the top spot. Although both of them were aware that they were part of the succession plan for the CEO position, it's interesting how their awareness influenced their behavior. One of the senior executives—I'll call him Bill—was inundated by the opportunity. It consumed him, and he was overwhelmed at the possibility of becoming the company's next CEO. Bill wanted the job badly, so he was fearful of doing anything that might put him at a disadvantage. His fear caused him to play things safe. Bill quit doing his senior executive job because he was so focused on the job he wanted. He stopped making decisions in his current role for fear that his decisions might be wrong and not achieve strong results. So he coasted, hoping not to screw up and hoping that the other senior executive in the running would. Bill was playing not to lose when he should have been helping his business win. When the time came to pick the next CEO, Bill missed out. His fear kept him from performing. He had become timid and spineless.

So what about the Anywhere Leaders? How do they remain determined and able to continue when they lose power and fear sets in? How do they remain objective when they grow in power? Well, as I said earlier, we all have a Zone of Objectivity. It's just that the Anywhere Leader's zone is bigger, wider (see Figure 6.2). The Anywhere Leader can deal with both lots of power and the loss of it.

You know these leaders. They are steady—never too high after a win and never too low after a loss. That doesn't mean they aren't passionate; they are. But they remain objective, knowing that if they aren't careful, they could grow too confident or become too cautious. These leaders have the distinctive ability to remain in a healthy state of objectivity because they recognize, and even manage, their own power punch.

The next two recommendations can help you remain determined by getting real with yourself and your circumstances.

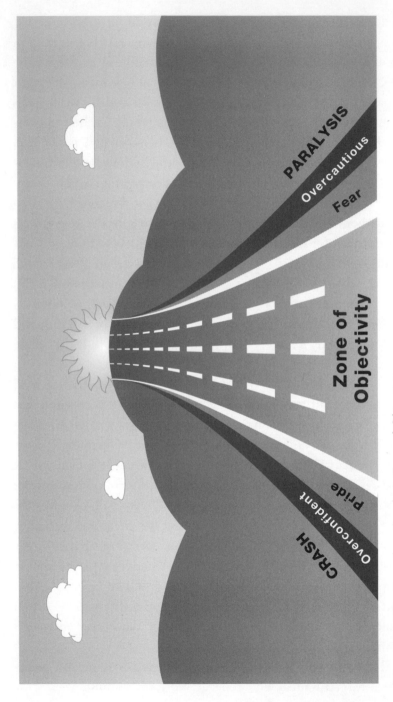

Figure 6.2 The Anywhere Leader's Zone of Objectivity

Recommendation #2: Take a Reality Check

To develop and sustain objectivity, you have to be realistic—about yourself, your abilities, and the circumstance you face. Let's begin with your self-perception. Anywhere Leaders fully realize, and may even tell themselves, that they aren't the best and they aren't the worst. Reminding yourself that you're not the best helps keep your arrogance in check and establishes some healthy humility. If you've never done a reality check or self-assessment, do it now.

Is there an area where you're a little too confident? Have you ever made a mistake due to arrogance? Or conversely, is your confidence significantly shaky in a particular area? If so, has it kept you from making a decision or moving forward? What about your prospects of failure or success? Are you realistic about those? How about your fears? Can you push them away with rational thinking, or are you stuck in panic mode? Fear can kill determination faster than anything else. But a good dose of reality goes a long way in overcoming it.

I have a major fear of spiders. My wife performs all the spider killings in our house. A psychologist friend of mine told me that one way to beat my fear was to contemplate the worst-case scenario of killing a spider. What if I missed the spider and it jumped on me? What if the spider bit me? What if I developed a nasty spider bite? What if, what if, what if? After I contemplated it all, after I imagined the worst, I could deal with the reality of spiders. By imagining the worst, I could ground my fear. Anywhere Leaders do this, too, when fear gets in their way. They go all the way with imagining the worst to arrive at a more realistic and objective view.

The ability to see the worst-case scenario is also a power check for the Anywhere Leader. She can imagine the crash that might occur if she becomes overconfident—and can realistically see the fallout. Not a pretty picture. She can also see the paralyzing affect that excessive cautiousness can have, and how indecision and doubt can lead to ruin. And last, she can imagine the real consequences of giving up. By fully understanding the reality of quitting, she develops a greater drive to continue.

As an Anywhere Leader, contemplate the realities of the situation. Imagine the "what ifs" behind the crash and behind the quit. Know that a crash or a decision to quit won't destroy you. But also come to grips with the reality that either one will have consequences that you'll want to avoid. Let your understanding of reality equip you to make the proper adjustments to keep you in the zone of objectivity.

Recommendation #3: Recognition and Restructuring

When I drive down a highway, the longer I travel, the more comfortable I get. The more comfortable I get, the faster I go and the more I start to let the car stray to the side. Most highways now have those bumpy grids on the shoulder that give you a warning that you're about to run off the road unless you change your direction. I have a love/hate relationship with those highway grid marks. I love them because they come in handy and give me a valuable warning. I hate them because their version of warning rattles my teeth.

Having mechanisms to alert you to impending danger is essential. Sticking with the automobile illustration, my tachometer warns me when I redline that I'm about to blow up my engine. My speedometer tells me how productive I am in getting to my destination. Anywhere Leaders know their key performance indicators (KPIs) behind their determination as well. They put measures in place that warn them when confidence is about to turn to arrogance and a dangerous outcome is looming. They recognize when they are being overcautious, even spineless, to the point of stagnation.

I have a few of these KPIs myself. I have an accountability team of three people who I meet with at least monthly. These three people give me direct and candid feedback—pointing out my blind spots and watch-outs. They keep my arrogance in check and will tell me when I am overconfident in something. They also let me know when they believe I've "checked out" of something incredibly important. This close team helps me stay within my zone of objectivity so that I can continue without a collapse. I have another team at home that keeps me grounded in reality—my family. My kids let me know in their sweet little way when I've ignored them or mismanaged my priorities.

I also have KPIs within my business. I've set up customer and employee feedback meetings where I can get valuable insight that helps me stay on track. I also have a 360-degree feedback report available at 36Dollar360.com that anonymously polls my direct reports, my peers, and my supervisors (customers) for their feedback about me. Additionally, I have our business results that show what's working and what's not working under my leadership.

I monitor these multiple KPIs to ensure that I'm receiving the most valuable and accurate information on my leadership. These KPIs help me make necessary adjustments and keep me operating in my zone of objectivity, helping me continue, determined, toward my aggressive goals.

What are your KPIs? If you don't have formal and informal tools that can provide you with valuable and accurate feedback on your leadership and on your performance, you run the risk of getting off track. Consider establishing feedback groups and 360-degree assessments to gain valuable feedback that can help you recognize and avoid some pretty significant pitfalls.

Anywhere Leaders don't just hear the warnings from their KPIs; they act on them. They are quick to restructure to make minor adjustments and even megashifts in their behaviors in order to remain valuable and productive. I'm around a lot of leaders who are sensationally committed to a balanced and controlled life. In my book *The Organizational Champion*, I dedicated a whole section to the myth of life balance for extraordinary people. In that book I talked about how life isn't a pie with six or eight equal slices. But, as leaders, we often believe that it is, and that if we aren't forking into all six or eight pieces on a regular basis, then we are letting ourselves and others down. A balanced life promises control, symmetry, and predictability. But the Anywhere Leader lives in uncertainty, not predictability. Balance is impossible in uncertain environments.

I don't want to be less than an extraordinary dad any more than I don't want to be a less than extraordinary executive. I want to be extraordinary in all aspects of my life; therefore, my life can't be six or eight equal slices of pie. When I have an important project with an aggressive deadline, I'm not balanced. I'm not home by five. I might even miss my daughter's performance at her school talent show. But I don't miss all of them. In fact, I hope to make most of those awe-inspiring events. And when I do, I'll be avoiding the cell phone and tomorrow's agenda altogether.

Early in my career, however, I struggled with this idea. I wanted to do it all. I even grew in my pride that I was the perfectly balanced person. Determined at work, joking with the family at home, beaming at the kids' recital, the picture of vitality on vacation, thoughtful in church, generous with my neighbors, dancing through the next chore, hedge clipping with a smile, tender at bedtime, and healthy as sin. I played the game of looking really good at being mediocre in everything I did. Maintaining it was impossible. And, of course, I started showing a few cracks. My KPIs started flashing the alarms. I wasn't happy, but rather, quite uncomfortable and edgy.

I made some significant adjustments. I restructured my approach in my relationships and in my day-to-day activities. I could no longer play the game, casting a disingenuous vibe. If I was going to work toward being extraordinary, I was going to have to be authentic. Today, I lead from a much more vulnerable platform. I'm okay with not knowing the answers. That wasn't true a few years ago, but then I got real with my family, real with my friends, and real in my business. And because of it, my joy increased significantly and so did my engagement in all aspects of life. My vulnerability gave me a new perspective: that I wasn't that big of a deal. When I realized that, I found new freedom, inspiration, and courage.

Based on your alerts and warnings, where and how should you restructure? What should you change in your approach, in your relationships, and in your day-to-day activities that will help you come off of the red line? What do you need to restructure to move to a more healthy state of mind and avoid the crashes or paralysis?

Your drive is dependent on your determination and your ability to persevere. Anywhere Leaders are committed despite the setbacks or challenges. They are able to remain objective, and therefore to continue, because their objectivity helps them avoid the crash and avoid paralysis. These leaders are self-aware and attuned with reality. They are ready to make the necessary effort to see things through. They recognize potential dangers that come from too much power or from having no backbone. And when they recognize potential dangers, they make adjustments that keep themselves productive and determined.

As you grow in power, keep in mind that power leads to arrogance, and arrogance leads to a crash. As you experience failure, keep in mind that failure leads to fear, and fear can remove you from the action completely. To remain more determined through power surges or periods of fear, keep these points in mind:

1. Grow your zone of objectivity.
2. Take a personal reality check.
3. Set up KPIs that help you recognize when your power is turning to arrogance or your failure is turning to fear.
4. Be willing to make changes in your life based on what the KPIs tell you.

Now let's look at how to develop curiosity.

Part Three

SENSATIONALLY CURIOUS

7

THERE IS MORE JOY IN KNOWLEDGE FOR THE ANYWHERE LEADER

C uriosity just might be the first emotion that we experience as infants. Even when we are in the womb, we are curious of the sounds we hear. When my wife was pregnant with our second child, she got on a pretty big ACDC kick (pun intended) and listened to the song "Back in Black"—a lot. If I had known how attentive Alex was, hanging out in my wife's belly, I might have suggested that we work in a little more Mozart, Bach, and Beethoven.

But even though we're born with a great amount of curiosity, Anywhere Leaders hunger for more and more knowledge and understanding because they gain a great amount of joy by learning and experiencing new things. They've experienced how their curiosity has set them up for greater success, so they develop even more of it. Those who lack curiosity often miss out on opportunities given to curious leaders—a lesson I learned the hard way.

From the time I was eight years old, I knew I wanted to fly fighter jets. When I was a teenager, I would park my car for hours at the end of runways and watch planes land, dreaming of the day that I'd be in the cockpit of a jet, tearing up the sky. And once I was in college I joined the Air National Guard to try to get a leg up in the pecking order of airmen competing for one or two pilot slots a year.

For six years I watched as other pilots took the slots that I was hoping for. I remember one guy in particular because even though he joined long after I did, we were up for the same slot. And it was my last shot at qualifying. At twenty-five, I was about to become too old for the military to invest in sending me to pilot school. If the selection came down to desire alone, I would have secured it in a heartbeat. A few weeks later, I found out that he got the slot and I didn't—the most significant blow in my life up to that point. Adding salt to my wound, I'd have to take care of his flight gear and assist him as he prepped for flight. Ugh!

Reflecting on that time, I can easily see how things unfolded in his favor. My mistake was that I kept my nose down, trying not to engage in personal politics. I did my job as a life support technician and survival instructor well, and I relied on my reputation as a hard worker to secure my spot. Meanwhile, the other guy immersed himself in the pilot world. He built strong relationships with other pilots, learned about their lives, invested time understanding their profession, participated in pilot culture, and asked lots of questions. While I sat back hoping to be discovered, he went off and discovered the job. Some people would say he was politicking for the position. He wasn't playing politics; he was gaining insight through his curiosity. He was becoming an Anywhere Leader—seeking knowledge in order to fit in and succeed in unfamiliar territory.

The advantage of the Anywhere Leader isn't found only in his ability to step up big to drive progress through his discerning, daring, and determined behavior, but also in his curiosity, which helps him maximize every morsel of information for exponential improvement and for new opportunities. Why? Because

Anywhere Leaders are more aware than most other people are, and know more than most others do. They connect more dots to a problem or opportunity because they've discovered more dots. Their curiosity makes them root-cause thinkers, getting deeper into the information than others who are attuned to only the surface issues.

While drive helps the Anywhere Leader achieve, what enables her to adapt to the unknown is her sensational curiosity—and her willingness to invest in the perspectives and practices of others. The Anywhere Leader never stops asking "What if?" and "Why not?" With the added strengths of being *reflective*, *receptive*, and *perceptive*, she's able to put what she discovers to good use. Those three strengths make her inclusive of others, and allow her to quickly connect, build trust, and gain respect.

The Anywhere Leader sees the individual strengths of her team members. She'll kick off a project by saying, "We have a ton to get done, and I want to know what your capabilities are before I throw you at something." Then she'll define the success of the mission in a way that is relevant to every person at every level, every step of the way. There is no way you can be a social klutz and still be an Anywhere Leader. To get your message heard, you have to know when and how to speak to different audiences. And you have to be able to size up people and situations at a glance, so that the minute you walk into a meeting or join a new team, you *get it.*

Being sensationally curious doesn't just extend to relationships, either. It's about seeking new experiences. It's about venturing beyond usual boundaries to see what's there—what's possible. Why do thousands and thousands of people climb Mount Kilimanjaro every year? Why do so many people plunge hundreds of feet into the ocean with oxygen tanks strapped to their backs? It's the same reason I learned to fly. It's the same reason President Kennedy wanted our country to explore the moon. Exploration is all about our need to know things we don't know.

Human beings are innately inquisitive, and we admire leaders who have the ability to take us into the unknown. But what we often get instead are people who want to lead us through the familiar and the predictable. In the known world, these leaders can look at the past and apply it to current and future times. They have every reason to be confident (and they usually are), because as long as nothing really changes, they have stability and security in their position. They bank on their title or stature to influence others, taking a "my way or the highway" stance. They protect the status quo and are scared to death of disruption.

I don't know. Maybe these leaders have found a tiny air pocket where business is certain and stable. But could they survive out in the real world, where uncertainty reigns? Not for long. Not without developing curiosity—and the desire to ask, listen, and adapt. Curious leaders eagerly move through uncharted waters where the risks are higher and so are the stakes. They are never satisfied with their knowledge; that's why they are consummate explorers. They aren't concerned about climbing corporate ladders; they're compelled to discover new vistas.

Why is that? What makes an Anywhere Leader so open to change and new ideas? One explanation comes from the innate curiosity that we all have. There is some science behind this, and it's important to understand how it works if you want to fully develop the trait. Curiosity is an emotion, and emotions are created and governed by the limbic system of the brain. That region produces a chemical called dopamine that creates the feeling of pleasure (think of it as brain candy). When chocoholics see a plate of triple fudge brownies, their brain releases dopamine. (We'll have more to say about dopamine later in the chapter.) The same happens when lovers spot each other across the room, or when your favorite song comes on the radio, or when you get that big promotion you've been waiting for. Interestingly, when the brain is exposed to certain types of intellectual stimuli, it releases the exact same chemical! Some people's brains are genetically coded to be more sensitive to intellectual stimuli than others. These people are naturally more curious and creative.

Before you counter with the excuse "I can't help it, my brain just isn't wired for curiosity," you should know that everyone has some degree of curiosity, and that those whose natural curiosity is low have the capacity to make up for the deficiency. The brain is sophisticated and can readily develop compensatory skills—which means you can readily develop your capacity for curiosity.

Neuroscience explains the roots of curiosity; behavioral science explains the actions that result from it. In a 2004 study, George Mason University psychologist Todd Kashdan uncovered two behavioral factors related to curiosity: *exploration*—the tendency to seek out novel situations and stimuli, and *absorption*—the tendency to become fully immersed in an interesting situation. It's a pretty basic relationship: We try new things and find that we enjoy the process of discovery—exploration. So then we spend more time living out the behaviors that get us closer to what we want to discover—absorption. We read more and ask more questions about the things that interest us or that we find enjoyable. We spend more time in contemplation and reflection. We gaze at something longer and look at it from different angles. And we find it fun to tinker with and test things.

So how does this relate to Anywhere Leadership? Simple. Curiosity builds awareness, awareness produces open-mindedness, and open-mindedness creates options. Psychologists refer to this as the "broaden and build" theory. The idea is that curiosity is a positive emotion, which means it helps expand our thinking toward new ideas. That broadening of thought allows us to build on our knowledge, skills, and resources. It makes us better equipped, both intellectually and psychologically, to overcome obstacles.

Negative emotions like fear do just the opposite: they narrow our thinking and shrink our view. When we're fearful, we consider only two options—stay and fight, or run. That's it. Only two. Fear limits our capacity and capability, whereas curiosity expands them—exponentially. It's the high-octane fuel for continuous learning, and leaders who possess it have a huge advantage over those who don't. Instead of locking up during stressful or uncertain times, curious leaders open up to new strategies and opportunities.

Curious people are highly *reflective*. When you catch them in thought, you can almost see their gears churning. In the past, we've idolized these people, making statues of them—most notably, Rodin's *The Thinker*. We celebrate them in music and poetry, but not so much in business. In business we don't want thinkers, we want doers. We expect answers and discount the thought process. We want those "quick on your feet" people. If we catch someone thinking, we want to know what's wrong, and what we can do to help get them back to work. In extreme cases you might even hear, "I don't pay you to think, I pay you to work."

Maybe that's why art is inspirational and business is operational. Inspiration requires time for contemplation. It's not the most productive process—it can't be. An artist sometimes has to wait for "it" to hit, but the business leader doesn't have the luxury of waiting. In business, productivity is everything. So are we to assume that reflection is a luxury that only artists can afford? Traditional thinking says yes, because business leaders are often punished for it. An overly reflective business leader is categorized as slower—in their work productivity and in their mental capacity. I'm just as guilty of this type of thinking as the next person, as I catch myself valuing the "get 'er done" leader over the perceived daydreamer.

Still, I myself like to spend time in reflection. But it isn't always easy. Even as I write this book, I mistakenly try to fast-track the ideas so that I can get to typing out the next two thousand words. At times like this, I have to remind myself "Slow down, Mike! Add a little reflection time in." To be an Anywhere Leader, you've got to strike a balance between thinking and doing. If you think too much, you may be overanalyzing or accepting an unproductive level of languor. However, if you move too quickly to action without much thought, you could be moving faster to disaster.

Curiosity has to start with reflection, because if it begins in dialogue with other people, the impact of your own experiences gets totally lost. Conversation takes over, and the agenda or experiences of colleagues, customers, or bosses move in. You risk losing your own references and instead try to relate to the experience of others—taking on their adventure and suppressing your own. When you lack that personal reflection time, you begin to lose your interest, your curiosity—which means less dopamine. Having a personal reference keeps curiosity relevant and makes it a little more interesting—more dopamine.

So next time you observe someone in contemplation and quiet reflection, consider giving the person a little grace—maybe even a little encouragement. Recognize that he is drawing from his own experiences to capture a solid reference point. He's finding ways to personally connect with, and take a greater interest in, the issue or challenge. He's searching and applying the most valuable source of knowledge—his personal experience—according to John Dewey, an influential philosopher of education. Realize that an element of inspiration brought about by related experience just might be necessary to solve a significant challenge—and reflection is the enabler of inspiration. Reflection doesn't require a mountaintop experience; it's just a matter of your relating past experiences to a new situation. And as important as reflection is, spending too much time in your own head is a problem. It's not enough to live your experiences; to become a sensationally curious Anywhere Leader, you have to connect with and process your experiences quickly. Once an Anywhere Leader has gone through her own vault of experiences that align with a particular issue or challenge, she then wants to know what others around her are thinking. And that's where the second strength—being *receptive*—comes in.

People who are highly reflective can be highly preoccupied with themselves. It's sometimes difficult for them to contemplate an idea or challenge and then share it with others. Not so with Anywhere Leaders. They have a distinctive ability to go deep with their own personal insights—calling upon their experiences, connecting with them, and forming some pretty strong opinions from them—yet put their egos aside and be open to the opinions of others. These leaders aren't afraid to shift their thinking. They are in pursuit of the best idea regardless of whether it comes from them or from someone else.

Their ability to be receptive to others elevates their ability to lead. Why? Because receptivity helps them connect and build trusted and valuable relationships. It helps them build favor with others: When someone likes me, I tend to like them back. When someone values me, I tend to value them back. My receptivity to others helps me be in community with them, and when I've effectively built community with others, I'm better equipped to perform and survive. I'm in a healthier state. This echoes Charles Darwin and his natural selection theory. Cooperators, being adaptable, live in a more healthy state and are more fit than "go it alone" dominators.

Receptivity offers another huge benefit to Anywhere Leaders, beyond its value for building relationships. It gives Anywhere Leaders greater knowledge. I can only live my own life and really relate to my own experiences. That limits me. The best leaders know how to draw upon the lives and experiences of thirty-seven other people. Within my own experiences, I have a few blind spots. But when I include others and their experiences, they help me make my unknowns known.

By being receptive to other people's input, I can even discover things that I didn't realize I knew. Someone once told me that I was a good listener. I always wanted to be a good listener, but until someone validated it for me, I assumed I needed lots of work to get there. But there are also things I can discover that I didn't realize I *don't* know. Boy, this can be humbling. If you're like me, then you've experienced a time or two, or more, when you've felt confident in your capability, only to have others point out how awful at it you really are. In church, I used to sing loudly. My own voice sounded really good to me. One day, my wife couldn't take it anymore and brought it to my attention that I'm not a very good singer. I didn't know this—I needed someone to point it out. Being receptive can really keep us from a great deal of embarrassment.

I'm a highly reflective person. And I like my ideas because they come from my experiences. This makes them personal to me. Therefore, when I invite others in to give their opinions, I'm prepping myself for a blow to the ego—I'm vulnerable to discovering my "unknown-unknowns." (That term came from U.S. Secretary of Defense Donald Rumsfeld when he was defending the decision to invade Iraq under the assumption that the country had weapons of mass destruction.) It's easy to shut down any discussion after forming my own opinion. But I must admit, without exaggeration, that when I have socialized a challenge and been receptive to the ideas of others after forming a strong personal opinion, the outcome has always been better. Always. Maybe in the end of contemplative process, 20 percent of a solution or direction might come from my reflection, and 80 percent might come from my reception of ideas from others. Maybe it's 50-50. Maybe it's 80 percent me and 20 percent them. Who cares? In the end, the best result won. The best results rarely, if ever, come from one person taking on all the burden of curiosity, while the others took on none.

To be truly receptive, you not only must be capable of receiving the input and advice of others, but you must also be ready and willing to put it to work. Think of it this way: If you work at a restaurant, you can easily pick up the phone and take a reservation. But if you don't secure the table and ensure that it is available for the guest, what's the point? Lots of leaders are open to receiving input, but they often have no intention of using it—right appearance, wrong motives. Although they want to appear as team players, you'll easily notice these unreceptive leaders because they end up doing all of the talking and none of the listening. The

Anywhere Leader seeks the input of others and then uses the good and effective ideas. In that way he's both conducive to, and conductive of, new ideas—and is willing to support and enable them.

To be that sensationally curious leader you must leverage your own experiences and insights (reflection), and the experiences and insights of others (reception) to increase your awareness, knowledge, and ability to make good decisions (perception). When you've reflected enough to exhaust your own ideas, and you've drawn upon others to capture their ideas, then you've broadened your knowledge and increased your awareness. You've captured all available insights and made new observations for greater understanding.

Having these insights and understandings makes you a *perceptive* leader—keenly aware and extraordinarily rare. Our big enterprise businesses need more perceptive people with the curiosity to quickly get up to speed. These businesses need leaders who can easily dial up a connection to the most challenging assignments by assessing the environment, gathering all available data, and obtaining the appropriate level of knowledge to lead. If you're not one of these people, then you likely hate them. They're the ones who come in after you and get the promotion ahead of you.

Looking back, I wish I had been much more aggressive in my approach to winning that pilot slot—talking to more people, asking more questions, growing my awareness, my insight, and my knowledge. People want to be known, and I need to know them. They want to be understood and appreciated. If you want to influence and ignite others, then ask for their ideas and use them. If you want to quickly solve a problem, then develop sensational curiosity about all aspects of the problem—the things at the surface and the things at the root. Reflect on the problem, gain new insights about it from others—know it. Then solve it. If you want to fit into a new culture that you've been assigned to, then grow your perception and awareness of that culture. Learn how to keep from being that social klutz that you read about. Develop your perception in order to fit in with a new team and a new culture. It's not about politicking; it's about taking a genuine interest in others. Realize the direction of your interest—you're interested in them, the results, and the collective success. You're not interested in their getting to know an idealized, overglamorized you. People can see right through your attempts to manipulate them in your personal favor.

Are you a genuinely and sensationally curious person? Are you spending enough time in reflection—drawing on your personal experiences and finding their relevancy to the situation you're facing? Are you drawing on the experiences and insights of others in order to broaden your knowledge? Are you genuinely open to the good ideas of others and willing to support and enable them, even if they challenge your thinking? Are you growing your knowledge with the right motives—for the sake of progress, not politics?

Develop more curiosity? How does anyone develop something so intangible?

For Anywhere Leaders, their curiosity is increased when they further develop their ability to be more *reflective*, *receptive*, and *perceptive*. I've talked about the three behavioral strengths of curiosity, starting with reflection—being open to one's own life experiences and willing to let these experiences influence your decisions. The question now is, how can I become a more reflective person?

8

BECOME REFLECTIVE

Every year, I take a vacation—by myself—without my wife and without my kids. I started taking this annual "me time" vacation seven years ago—and even though my wife doesn't go with me, she cherishes them. So do my coworkers. Even my kids appreciate them. When I come back, I'm a much better husband, a much better dad, and a much better boss.

I call these annual vacations my own Radical Sabbatical. I must confess that, when I started taking these trips, I took a lot of heat from my friends. They wondered how I could be so selfish and why I wanted to be alone. Some of them would just wink at me and say, "Lucky dog. I wish I could garner some of that me time."

But these personal Radical Sabbaticals aren't just any vacation. I plan in some extremes. For my Radical Sabbaticals, I get completely lost, completely alone, and completely bored—landing in some pretty sparse locations. While planning one of my trips to Costa Rica, I didn't dial up the W Hotel in one of the bigger cities.

I spent the entire time under the trees on the side of a mountain—feeling very lonely and very lost. Even in one of the most beautiful places on Earth, I found myself a little bored after three or four days. But it's when boredom sets in and when things get very quiet that my body and mind start to recharge.

These annual trips are important to me because I come out of the experience physically and spiritually restored and intellectually alive. My curiosity is at an all-time high. My own Radical Sabbatical forces me to contemplate and reflect on some really important things.

Reflection is the thinking process behind curiosity—the internal acquisition of knowledge. Curiosity begins with reflection because it stems from our own observations and experiences, not someone else's. Therefore, our reflection is dependent on our experiences. The most reflective people in life seem to have had a whole lot of life experiences.

John Dewey, the influential philosopher of education, believed that only through experience does man learn about the world—and only through experience does he maintain and better himself in the world. Dewey argued that our schools did not provide genuine learning experiences, but only an endless amassing of facts that were fed to the students, who spat them back from their short-term memory and then promptly forgot them. Where was Dewey's philosophy when I went to college and crammed my mental bank with memorization?

Dewey describes the difference between real learning and book learning. Personal experience adds perspective, tone, feel, and emotion to the knowledge. We learn more by sailing the seven seas than we do by reading about them or hearing about them from others. Our experiences equip us to be reflective—to consider our own observations. We do something, experience the outcome of our behavior, reflect on the consequences, and then capture the knowledge. The experience gives learned knowledge relevance to our lives. And the relevance makes it "sink in."

I learned more about cancer by watching my mom and my son battle it, and ultimately lose their lives to it. I saw when doctors became hopeless, and when my mom and my son grew gravely weak. I saw how hard chemotherapy is on the body and how limited we are in our fight against cancer. My dad is no doctor; he's an ex-military officer. But like me, he experienced the significant impact of cancer through his wife and grandson. He hadn't been formally educated in oncology. But he experienced it firsthand, and from his experience, he has written a compelling book, titled *A New Strategy for the War on Cancer*. Despite his lack of "formal" qualifications, my dad is getting rave reviews and support by top oncologists around the world.

When I began writing this chapter, I didn't start off practicing what I preached. Instead, I immediately started to read research publications and talk to some of the experts who had some really good points. Sure, I wanted their influence, but not without my first wrapping my own brain around the concept from my own experiences. So allow me to try and answer the question "How does one become more reflective?" by reflecting on the question myself.

Recommendation #1: Make Your Own Adventures

I want to be careful not to minimize this point—being reflective means to take on more of your own knowledge adventures, *not* to read about the knowledge adventures of others. Anywhere Leaders don't just read more stuff, they *do* more stuff. They're "book smart" to a degree, but they don't bank on book knowledge. These leaders don't look to the book or reference guide and then call it a day. They get to the experience.

Reflection is just plain impossible without firsthand experience. Howard Hughes, who brought major innovations to the film and aviation industries, had his personal struggles, but no one can argue that he was one of the most broadly successful people in history.

Hughes seemed to have had his hands in just about everything. When his company designed new aircrafts, he wanted to be the test pilot, not ship that job off to someone else. Hughes immersed himself in every experience.

Like many other wildly successful people, Hughes also dropped out of college—like Steve Jobs, Bill Gates, Walt Disney, Henry Ford, John Rockefeller, and thousands of others. These wildly successful leaders pursued the experience and the adventure and gained firsthand knowledge. I'm not diminishing the value of an education. I highly value it because of the perspective it gives and its ability to broaden the student's understanding of things. Education can make you more receptive—a critical element of curiosity. It's just that education should not replace experience. The classroom shouldn't replace the expedition. But it often does, and we as leaders settle for it—thereby diminishing our reflective temperament.

Your ability to be reflective is directly tied to your ability to experience. People who get out and do more, who go places and see more firsthand, are going to have more to reflect on than those who limit themselves to the library, the living room, and the movie theater. Leaders who find significant value in their reflection are in pursuit of the experience.

Next time you find yourself needing to do some investigation or needing to increase your knowledge, don't start by racing to the bookstore to see what some author has to say. Don't start by running to the experts to hear their take. Like Anthony Stark, the fictional character in the movie *Iron Man*, make the trips to the front lines of the battle and get immersed in the experience; you'll find an extraordinary perspective there. Stark's invention of the miniaturized arc reactor happened from his reflection that was enabled by his firsthand experience.

Do you have the necessary experience to make a sound decision on an important issue? If not, consider capturing a basic overview of the challenge or opportunity, and then put yourself in the ring.

If you're asked to create a digital marketing plan using social media, then get your own Twitter account, contribute to a blog and leave comments, become a fan of a business on Facebook, participate in a webinar, and pick out a few favorites for your Internet browser. If you're asked to assess the opportunity to open up a new market segment for a product, then go beyond data mining the demographic reports. Live the market segment—buy what they buy, taste what they taste, live where they live, do what they do.

Your experience will better prepare you for valuable reflection and make you much more capable of contemplating the "what ifs" and "why nots."

Recommendation #2: Diversify Your Experiences

Do one thing really well—but do lots of other things, too. Anywhere Leaders don't just have a lot of experiences to draw on in their reflection; they also have a broad base of diverse interests and diverse experiences to draw on. Bill Gates is said to have an interest in the economy, chemistry, medicine, and linguistics. His mind contemplates topics beyond pure business.

Anywhere Leaders may have a few hobbies and interests — second languages, science, sports, nutrition, and travel. Some of these hobbies may even be a little strange: take Digital Space founder and CEO Bruce Damer, who raises pot-bellied pigs. These interests and hobbies help leaders develop broader experiences. In my business, I've reflected on and learned from sports, travel, sailing, flying, and writing. These broad experiences give me distinctive insights and perspectives on business challenges. I can get outside of my business mind and draw from some parallel occurrences. Writing helps me reflect on business trends that, without that discipline, I likely would have ignored. Sports helps me plan against our competition. My reflection on my flying experience helps me better calculate and contemplate risk. Sailing helps me be much better at preparation.

Variety and broad-based experiences can give a leader a wealth of distinct perspectives and insights. The variety also helps give Anywhere Leaders more "Aha!" moments and surprising revelations. Think about it—today's vertically minded specialists with years of experience are seldom caught off guard. They've invested years in making sure things are pretty much predictable. A long-time police officer has likely seen it all. A painter who does all her work in oils knows exactly how to tame the canvas. A twenty-year logistics manager can move the packages in his sleep. If intense specialists aren't careful, they run the risk of falling into a mundane routine and a rote mindset.

It's hard to be reflective in the rote. Rote is mechanical and repetitive. In contrast, Anywhere Leaders are ready and eager for the "Aha!" moments, the surprises, the challenges, the uncertainty. They know that when they face new challenges, a generalist mindset with multiple reference points can help them better navigate the unknown without getting locked up. Vertical specialists are extremely uncomfortable with the unpredictable; Anywhere Leaders are prepared for it. Their broad experiences have prepped them to remain steady in most any environment.

To increase your ability to be reflective, seek different types of experiences and do a few different things. If your life resembles a Norman Rockwell painting (everyday-life scenarios in Middle America), it's time to splash it with a little abstract art. If your life is basically predictable—a morning cup of coffee with the morning paper, a rote job, a ten-minute commute home, a well-balanced dinner, news at 6 o'clock, and asleep before 10 o'clock—consider taking up something entirely new: racquetball, a vacation, a reading group, wine tasting, rock climbing, cooking, anything that can introduce a new experience that gives you new perspective for reflection. Then connect these experiences with current issues or challenges.

Ask yourself, *What did I learn from an argument I had at a racquetball game that can help me deal with a heated conversation at work?* When you got stung by that jellyfish on the beach during vacation, how did you maintain your poise without losing it in front of your kids? When you met with your reading group, why was the collaboration so rich—and why can't you get the same thing from your work team? When you're at your next executive meeting, recall and order that new Cabernet Sauvignon you tasted last week.

By having a variety of experiences, you're creating an encyclopedia in your brain. You can be your own search engine. You know enough about lots of things to be interesting. And those things that you know enough about can be very valuable thought starters to some very valuable solutions.

Recommendation #3: Set Aside Time to Think and Brainstorm Alone

On a recent road trip by myself to Little Rock, I saw a beautiful German shepherd walking along the side of the highway. That observation triggered a memory of my childhood pet German shepherd named Jet. The recall of the memory inevitably led to contemplation. *Why are they called German shepherds? Are they really from Germany? I wonder what Jet would have acted like around sheep?* An hour later—but feeling like it had been only a few minutes—I was at my destination. My mind had wandered in a single thought pattern because nothing else was there to fill it.

For Anywhere Leaders, such times are rare—that's precisely why they make the effort to seek them out. More often it seems as if our brains are jumping around through a dozen issues at once. Those are the times when our brains feel full—like we can't pack in any more information. It's fairly impossible to get reflective when our heads are full. Reflection happens when a person goes deep in thought to capture new insights or revelations. That's what Anywhere Leaders do. They allow themselves to go deep in thought. And even though it may sound a little weird, they actually have conversations with themselves—though not neces-sarily out loud.

Reflection is different from daydreaming. Daydreaming is divergent and tangential; reflection is fully focused on a target topic or idea. Daydreaming is not a deep single pattern of thought, but rather a very random pattern of thought. Daydreaming is effortless and unproductive; reflection contemplates real and rel-evant issues and ideas.

The point is, to become more reflective, Anywhere Leaders set aside some time to simply think thoughts. They have to intention-ally set this time, because these times don't often just come by happenstance throughout their days.

Are you allowing your mind to get deeply into thought? Are you intentional about sectioning off time for contemplation? Keep focused on a single thought, idea, or topic so that you don't go into daydreaming. If you're concerned that this idea sounds extremely unproductive, consider the value consequence of losing a good thought. To counter the urge to fill up every open space in your mind, start your contemplation accompanied by a journal or blank sheet of paper to keep you in the right mindset for contemplation. I have several friends who do this—and their journals are some of their most prized possessions.

Recommendation #4: Move Closer to the Edge Without Going Over It

I talked about this idea in Chapter Five when I discussed develop-ing a more *daring* nature. But it's worth briefly highlighting again in this section. Pushing for progress puts us out there. We have to be somewhat daring to get difficult things started. We have to push harder and go further. You may have heard the saying, "If it were easy, everyone would do it." Anywhere Leaders are bold and brave, driving the difficult things.

But for this discussion, it's important to communicate the personal value you gain from being a little bolder and a little braver—to motivate you to push yourself further than you normally would. These bold and brave moves serve as personal tests that lead to personal discovery. Whenever I have made a bold move and succeeded, I've learned so much more about myself and my capabilities. And whenever I've made a bold move and failed, I've still learned so much more about myself and my capabilities. Either way, pushing myself, sometimes close to the edge, has given me incredible insights and perspective. I have learned more and recalled more from those "close to the edge" moves than I ever have from the moves that nicely fit within my known capabilities.

I was close to the edge when I accepted a large project that stretched our organizational capacity. I had to weigh the organizational pressures against the benefit of a very large piece of business. The risk was that we would fail if our organization was incapable of stretching—even if we worked harder than we already were. Such a stretch taught me a lot about our people and our capabilities. Our organization showed that it could do more. Our people showed confidence and resilience. We grew our knowledge, and we became tighter as a team. And we delivered. My curiosity had wanted to know what we were capable of. By pushing us to the edge, I found out that we were a whole lot more capable than I had originally thought—a very valuable insight for future planning.

I never forget my "close to the edge" actions. When I reflect on them, I'm better equipped to contemplate the uncertainty of what's ahead. I know just how far I think I could go, and I wonder what it will take to go just a little further—to push things just a little further—slight tweaks and adjustments, stemming from reflection, that make all the difference in the world in the competitive landscape.

As you develop your own ability to be more reflective, realize that the reflective process is an internal search of your experiences. Therefore:

- Make more of *your* own adventures for the sake of making more memories—do more stuff.

- Diversify *your* experiences so that you have a broader base of memories to draw on as *you* contemplate issues. Do lots of different stuff. Add a little variety in your life to gain more perspective and gain more insights that *you* can apply.

- Invest more of *your* time into thinking through *your* own thoughts.

- Push *yourself* a little closer to the edge—taking things a little further than *you* normally would—to stretch and test *yourself* more.

When making decisions, do much more reflecting. Build up your brain encyclopedia so you can draw on a lot of those things you know just enough about. Increase your ability to be reflective by doing more and seeing more—putting yourself in the ring, helping yourself contemplate your actions in the face of uncertainty.

Your reflection is enormously valuable to your leadership, and my bet is that it's not used nearly enough in your leadership. Anywhere Leaders spend a lot of time in reflection. So should you.

Oh, and one more thing. Consider taking your own personal Radical Sabbatical in the near future.

9

BECOME RECEPTIVE

Although we start by being reflective as we process our curiosity, we certainly don't end there. Reflection is only the beginning. Anywhere Leaders are also highly receptive. It is essential to find the right moment to be reflective and the right moment to be receptive. Let's start there, at the tension between reflective and receptive behaviors, before we dive into how to develop an ability to be more receptive.

Anywhere Leaders aren't balanced between reflective and receptive, with one side being reflective and the other being receptive on a balance scale. They don't strive for the proper or healthy balance of reflection mixed with the right amount of receptiveness. When Anywhere Leaders are reflective, they are fully immersed in their reflection. They give their reflection time 100 percent of their attention. They fully process it in their minds and give anything that comes out of their reflection the time needed to fully ripen. These leaders make sure that they go all the way with the period of reflection, deploying their full mental capabilities. Once they've data-mined everything they've got about an idea, an opportunity, or a challenge, *then* they switch gears and transition into vetting their ideas with others and capturing ideas from them; this transition marks the move into a receptive mindset. Once that occurs, they are fully immersed in listening to the ideas, insights, and experiences of others.

Managing reflection and reception isn't a matter of balance; it's a process. Reflection is the first step, as we process new ideas and thoughts brought about through our curiosity. Being receptive is the second step. Anywhere Leaders do a healthy amount of reflecting before they open up to the ideas of others. They don't come empty-handed to a conversation. They come fully equipped to engage, discuss, and even debate when moving into receptivity. Contrast that to the person who shows up to a meeting having given zero thought to any of the issues that need to be discussed and debated.

Being fully reflective allows you to confidently move forward to being fully receptive. So how do you increase your ability to become more receptive? You become more poised, you create a receptive environment, and you proactively seek out the insights of others.

Recommendation #1: Bring the Right Attitude to the Discussion

Today's leaders can't afford to be closed-minded know-it-alls. Maybe you could get away with your closed-minded nature twenty or thirty years ago, but not today. Closed-minded know-it-all leaders are following the fate of the dinosaurs in the current business environment. And they stand out in businesses like a Tyrannosaurus in a flowery meadow. These leaders are quick to bite when disagreement arises in the conference room. They collaborate only when they are forced to. What they don't realize is how much of a disadvantage they are creating for themselves. These know-it-all leaders easily become isolated after awhile. What they perceive to be signs of strength—firm voice, commanding presence, lack of patience, fearless scowl—become signs of weakness over time. They are the dominators who are struggling to operate with cooperators. Eventually, dominators die and cooperators thrive.

Anywhere Leaders aren't dominators. They bring a different attitude to workplace interactions: the right attitude for receptiveness. Sure, Anywhere Leaders love their ideas. After all, they are passionate leaders who are personally invested. But these leaders just don't take someone's disagreement or different point of view so personally. They don't view differing opinions from others as threats. They don't easily get rattled when someone shoots holes in their ideas. They are able to cognitively soften their defenses. How? By being hyperaware of the natural human tendency to protect the ego and by adjusting their behavior to counter that natural tendency. Some people pull this off by counting to ten before they respond—making sure their responses aren't purely reactive, but rather thought through a little more. Some people bite their tongues, giving themselves time to sit with their thoughts a little more. When I'm debated, I pay close attention to my nonverbal cues, trying to control them so that I come off a little more open and encouraging in how I'm perceived—even though internally I may feel like my ego is taking a beating.

Anywhere Leaders know that defenses create barriers to improvement and betterment. They know that their tendency will be to defend their position, so they come to discussions and interactions trying less to be the authority and trying more to be the engaged student who seeks answers, discussion, and constructive debate.

Ask yourself:

- *Do I come to meetings wanting to be right or wanting to learn more?*

- *Do people perceive me as open to the ideas of others in my interactions, or do others feel that I dominate the discussion?*

- *Am I patient about offering comments, or do I race to contribute?*

If you're like me, you're probably asking yourself, *How do I maintain the mindset of a leader, and yet position myself as a student— eager to learn?* Therein is a significant key to being an Anywhere Leader. These leaders manage such a paradox well. Consider the following steps as you work to bring the right attitude to a discussion or interaction with others.

As you approach a discussion or interaction, first make sure you *orient for improvement*. Realize that improvement—not winning the debate—is the goal in the discussion. People who *orient themselves for improvement* seek out better ideas from others and ask them more questions. They prize progress, not self-gratification.

Once you've oriented yourself for improvement by setting the right goals or objectives for the discussion, then *present the right presence*. This means that as a leader you must consciously manage your verbal and nonverbal communications. Emotionally intelligent leaders do this well. When emotionally intelligent people have a curiosity directed toward improvement and therefore want to be receptive to the ideas of others, they don't show up at the conversation table pounding their fists and demanding performance. They don't show up with an angry scowl suggesting that everyone should be on guard. Theirs is a poised presence. They appear comfortable and steady. They appear eager and interested. They ask lots of open-ended questions and actively participate in the discussion. Their presence helps make open discussion feel safer and more comfortable.

Once you've presented the right presence, then *encourage the exchange of ideas*. Reinforce the fact that people are at the table because they bring something to it. Ask people to actively participate, and tell them that you expect to see their involvement and contribution. Be careful not to shut down others when you may have a different view. It may sound elementary, but comments such as "That's so stupid" or "I think you're way off base and out of touch" can bring any conversation to a halt. Even those people who had been on target and in touch with their thoughts will be negatively impacted and less participative when encouragement stops and judgment starts.

Finally, to bring the right attitude to the discussion, *nurture your novice nature*. As you approach these meetings, remind yourself to play the role of a student. Be an eager learner in such interactions and encounters. You will get much more value out of the discussion or interaction if you play the role of a sponge and not a brick wall.

In order to process their curiosity by using receptivity, Anywhere Leaders bring the right attitude to any discussion or interaction. They do this by being OPEN. You can do the same if you:

Orient for Improvement

Present the right presence

Encourage the exchange of ideas

Nurture your novice nature

Recommendation #2: Beware of Dogma

Being receptive counters entrenched dogma. Our dogmatic nature can become entrenched when we start and stop with what we know; when we look only into ourselves and to our own experiences, or look only inside our organizations. Our dogmatic nature makes us blind to things evolving around us, and fosters inflexible, rigid, and narrow-minded thinking and decision making. We fail to keep up, and we fall behind. We stop with our idea and don't think it can improve. A dogmatic mindset often settles in when we are reflective and not receptive.

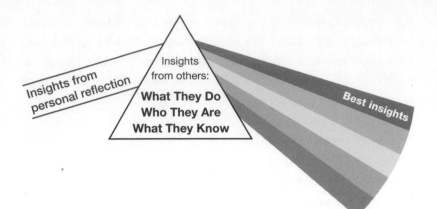

Figure 9.1 The Insight Prism

I love using the image of a light beam passing through a prism to communicate how reception helps our ideas become more vibrant and interesting. Consider your reflection—your brought-in thoughts from your own experiences—to be a light beam. A light beam is usually pure white. Consider receptiveness—your openness to the ideas, experiences, and perspectives of others—to be the prism. For the illustration in Figure 9.1, I've added labels to the prism to represent important elements for broadening our view for a more vibrant and interesting outcome. These elements are shown in the figure and described shortly.

This model illustrates how engaging others creates more value. It shows how your own insights interact with the insights of highly engaged colleagues to co-create better, more enduring insights. From many minds come stronger ideas and stronger minds: that's why Anywhere Leaders invite others into the discussion and allow them to contribute. These others bring in their own social context, established by their environment and from the personal relationships they have. These others bring in who they are as a person—physically and psychologically. They bring in the knowledge that they've gained from their experiences, and they bring in what they do, which gives them a unique reference point. When we are receptive, we gain insights that take us beyond dogmatic and limited thinking. By being receptive, our insights are expanded and enhanced, as illustrated in Figure 9.1.

To protect against your dogmatic nature, learn to socialize your ideas more. But don't invite others in just for input and discussion; invite lots of different people in with different perspectives. Talk with people who are older and younger than you. Get input from people who think differently from you, and view them as valuable, not as a threat. Reach across boundaries and borders to vet and debate your ideas or to find some entirely new ones.

It's easy. In fact, what's harder today is finding an excuse for not being receptive. You've got to work to keep private. By pressing a few buttons on my computer or phone, I can poll over three hundred people on my Facebook page. I sent Jimmy Fallon, the popular late-night talk show host, a message on Twitter just minutes ago. Our networks and our reach stretch so much further today than ever before (what an understatement!). Anywhere Leaders make use of them.

If you're leading behind a guarded desk and shunning the majority of your opportunities for interactions, you're moving toward irrelevance and atrophying in your own ideas. Get out more and get in touch with more people. Be open to their influence to defend against your dogmatic nature.

What is keeping you from making the most of your personal network? Are you concerned that your ideas are not strong enough to stand on their own, so you go to only people who are exactly like you and will likely validate your own limited assumptions and results? Are you open to honest criticism, or are you only "going through the motions"?

Recommendation #3: Make Time for Collaboration

One of the biggest barriers to getting involvement and ideas from others is the aggressive timelines and due dates of projects or initiatives. Often we feel like we don't have time to inquire across a diverse network of people. Because of the time constraints, we feel that we're forced to go it alone. So it is important that you plan into your projects specific times for review, discussion, and collaboration. By planning for receptiveness and collaboration, you won't miss the opportunities to capture valuable insights from others. We all do what we plan to do. A plan without time budgeted for collaboration and discussion is an inadequate plan. Next time you plan your project, ensure that you set milestone intervals with time for collaboration and reviews. It's a simple action that can help you be more intentional about your receptivity.

Recommendation #4: Create a Receptive Environment

There's a problem with how easily connectable we are with society. Although our ability to connect with others gives us an advantage as we try to capture new ideas and insights from others, such accessibility also presents a major challenge. When you're asked to provide input and insights, that's the time to be accessible to the person who's right there, requesting your time—not the time to be accessible to the entire world.

When you're in a collaborative meeting that promotes the exchange of ideas, it isn't the time or place to update your status on Facebook or participate in an irrelevant online discussion. If you're like me, you've attended meetings where mobile devices and computer buzzers and dings are going off constantly. What's more, each little ding spurs all the attendees to start digging through pockets for mobile devices. So much for a productive meeting! To create a receptive environment, you may have to go to extremes—I know I have. There are meetings where I just don't allow computers, and I encourage people to leave their phones at their desks. For such meetings, you should seek the full attention of the attendees and work to block out the distractions. Next time you want a high level of contribution from meeting participants, ask them to leave their devices at their desks. It will help you focus more productively and increase the level of contribution.

It's also important that your company culture communicate a need for open and ongoing collaboration. For this reason, companies all over have installed open floor plans. They've redesigned their office furniture and office space to create more opportunities for people to connect. Pods and working tables are now office staples. There are fewer doors in the most innovative and collaborative offices. Even if your offices are full of walls, narrow halls, and corner offices, you can still create an open and collaborative working environment. To overcome an old or bad office design and instill a collaborative culture, you'll need to get out of your seat and walk the halls a whole lot more. You'll need to be comfortable making pop-in visits to other offices with doors and walls. You'll also need to get more comfortable receiving such visits.

Pop-ins are common in open environments. Today's collaborative workers know how to deal with them and remain productive, because, in most instances, a connected workplace is more productive than one that prioritizes privacy. Don't allow walls to keep you from connecting—walk the halls.

What does your office environment or company culture say? For formal meetings that demand the contribution of participants, block out the distractions and make sure attendees are fully committed and engaged. For informal collaboration that comes from a collaborative culture, make sure your office environment is structured and designed in a way that doesn't alienate people, but rather brings them together.

As a recap to increasing your ability to become more receptive, consider performing the following:

- Bring the Right Attitude to the Discussion: Be
  OPEN—Orient for improvement, Present the right
  presence, Encourage the exchange of ideas, and
  Nurture your novice nature.

- Beware of Dogma—Seek out the ideas and input of diverse others, allowing them to improve and progress your ideas further to make them interesting and vibrant.

- Make Time for Collaboration—Don't just plan the functional components of a project; plan in your stakeholder reviews and collaboration meetings as well.

- Create a Receptive Environment—View collaboration in two ways: formal and informal. For formal collaboration, set up the environment to protect against distractions. For informal collaboration, make sure your office structure works to create more conversations among employees: connecting them, not isolating them.

10

BECOME PERCEPTIVE

I often wonder what it must have been like in the cockpit of U.S. Airways Flight 1549 that crash-landed in the Hudson River. I know that the pilot, Captain Chesley Sullenberger, talked a lot afterward about how his training prepared him for such a disaster, but a training manual and a simulation are surely different from the real thing. I'm sure Sullenberger's awareness was at an all-time high and his senses were fully alert on January 15, 2009, when his plane lost power over New York City. He may have relied on a strong cup of coffee to sustain him in training as he thumbed through the manual. No coffee was needed when a flock of Canada geese collided with both jet engines of the Airbus 320. I imagine Sullenberger's eyes were wider and his ears were more attuned than normal. I'm sure he felt every tiny little bump on his descent—feeling turbulence to which he was usually oblivious.

It's the same for Anywhere Leaders facing uncertainty—though thankfully not quite to the same degree. All of us have a heightened awareness when we find ourselves in unfamiliar and uncertain situations. To better deal with such uncertainty, Anywhere Leaders have developed greater perception and greater awareness than others.

What do we mean by perception, and why is it important? For the Anywhere Leader, perception is akin to awareness. It is the ability to see the bigger picture without sacrificing the quality of resolution that makes it possible for us to zoom in and focus on the details when necessary. Let's look at what developmental brain science shows us about sensory impressions. Much of the science focuses on the perception capabilities of children. Infants come into the world incapable of perceiving very much. They are clumsy and almost completely unaware. They fall, burn themselves, knock things off the shelf, bonk themselves on the head, pull the ear of a not-so-friendly dog, and pour their milk all over important documents. But as these infants grow, they start to develop the ability to take in information from their senses. They learn about consequences. They develop a cognitive awareness to not pull the dog's ear or the dog might bite and hurt. They try not to spill the milk because they know Mom will get angry. They don't touch the stove because they know it will burn their fingers— they've done it before.

Infants start to develop a greater ability to perceive within three months. But development doesn't stop there. Every encounter we have contributes to even greater perception and more awareness.

So far, in understanding how we process our curiosity, we've discussed how becoming more reflective of our experiences sparks more useful and relevant insights. We've also talked about how becoming more receptive to others opens us to gain those external insights. When we combine our reflection and our reception, we become more aware and more keenly dialed in—in short, more perceptive. In this section, we will address another important aspect of perception: using all our senses to survive and thrive in radically new circumstances and during surprising turns of events.

Sensory perception is vital to Anywhere Leaders, because they often find themselves in uncertainty—that is, in situations where they have no experience to recall. They find it hard to draw parallels from previous experiences because previous experiences just don't exist. But their senses feed their curiosity and help them adapt and learn fast.

When I was in the military's prisoner of war camp training in the middle of who knows where, I had no experience in my life to draw from. Nothing else was like this experience—there was no room for reflection. Not only was I cut off from the world, but even if I could inquire of some of my comrades, they wouldn't have a clue what to do either. No reflection, no reception, but still—I was anxiously curious about what was coming—what would happen to me. After all, these "training" captures were surprisingly rough, and the conditions were shocking.

Being more alert to my senses would have to carry me through this ordeal. I would have to be highly attentive during such extreme uncertainty. My eyes would have to determine what was available to me. Food? (Cold oatmeal on the floor.) Blankets? (Unh-uh.) Toilet? (Hardly—a tin can.) My ears would have to listen. *Any friends around?* (Nope.) *Does anyone speak my language?* (Unh-uh—just lots of yelling.) My skin would tell me when I was getting too cold. You get the point. Lacking reference points or parallels, my senses would have to be on full alert. My senses, not my experiences or the experiences of others, would be my guide. To determine who I could trust and who I needed to stay away from, my own emotional intelligence would be vital.

When Anywhere Leaders land in uncertain circumstances with no experience to call upon, they know how to open and heighten their senses and sharpen their external focus. They become amazingly observant and keenly aware of their surroundings. When an Anywhere Leader lands in a new culture, he is more alert to even

the subtlest behaviors and undertones. When meeting administra-
tors punt on an established agenda and shift in a surprisingly new
direction, Anywhere Leaders don't check out, but rather listen
even more intently. When Anywhere Leaders make a necessary
decision with hardly enough information, they don't cross their
fingers in hopes of a good outcome. These leaders grow more
attentive—keeping an eye or ear out for any piece of information
that might clue them in to how their decision is playing out in
case an adjustment is necessary.

So, how can you heighten your awareness, your perception,
during times of uncertainty? In a sentence, first by drawing on past
experiences—reflection; then by drawing on the insights and experiences of others—reception; and then by being more in tune with
your senses. The rest of this chapter provides recommendations for
how you can become more perceptive.

Recommendation #1: Learn More and Know More

Were you one of those people who couldn't wait to graduate from
high school or college because you were so sick of learning and
battling a lack of motivation due to senioritis? I was. I couldn't
wait to get out of school and start working in a real job. Hadn't I
learned enough? The rude awakening as I began my career was that
"doing work" meant more and more learning.

The continuous learners in the workplace are the ones who
seem to get ahead. They are never done learning; rather, they are
eager to tackle some new challenge that forces them to learn
something new. They are in pursuit of every piece of knowledge
and every insight. These continuous learners are easy to spot.
They're the ones in your organization who listen well, who take
lots of notes, and who don't wait for annual reviews to seek out
feedback from others. They are very observant people who want
to be a part of conversations. They are involved and engaged with
others—but not necessarily for the social value they receive. Some

of these learners just might be serious introverts. They are involved because they are curious.

Compare the continuous learner with the employee who shows up in the morning and leaves at the end of the day without notice. These employees are hard to spot, as they don't make much noise and are often zoned out inches from the computer monitor. When they do glance away and get up from the desk, it's usually to take a lunch break. I know that I'm in danger of overgeneralizing. I realize that some jobs call for zoned-out monitor gazers—not all jobs can be Anywhere Leader jobs. But the point is that continuous learners are involved leaders who proactively seek out lots of information and are tapped into a number of resources—business reports, compelling articles, developmental books, and a few advisers and experts.

Which one are you? Do you go somewhat unnoticed throughout your day? If so, it is important for you to find ways to get involved in the conversation and to tap into resources that give you new insights. It's hard to contemplate things when there is nothing there for you to contemplate! Continuous learners put themselves in a position to tap into more resources so that they can contemplate more things. The perceptive leader is a continuous learner with lots of informational inputs that feed her knowledge.

To stay up with current knowledge, I have a number of knowledge inputs myself. I learn from a number of advisers, I subscribe to about ten insightful publications, I have RSS feeds that push information to my email inbox, I'm an involved member of our industry's professional organization, and I am constantly pushing myself into a number of conversations just to stay involved. And all of it is for the sole purpose of learning enough to remain sharp.

Are you a continuous learner who is keeping up with knowledge? Assess your knowledge inputs. Do you have enough? If so, are you accessing and using them to keep your mind sharp?

Recommendation #2: Focus on the Essentials

Have you ever found yourself in a crowded airport where you can barely hear the boarding call? If so, when your flight number was called amidst all the noise, you've probably edged closer and turned your ear toward the announcer to hear better. You may have even closed your eyes to block out other senses so that you could focus on just listening.

Leading in unpredictable, unfamiliar, and uncertain environments can sometimes add more "noise clutter" to our job, making it harder to focus on the important things. An athlete experiences something similar when he makes it to the next level of competition. In each transition, you might hear him talk about how the game is so much faster than at the previous level. But after awhile, the game starts to slow down for the athlete. Why do you think that is? We all know that the game doesn't really slow down. What has happened is that the athlete has become more comfortable and more familiar in his role. What was once unfamiliar to him has now become very familiar. He's no longer surrounded by all of the noise clutter.

Athletes develop cognitive heuristics that help them to shut out certain things—unimportant things—and to pay attention to the important stuff. And as they make the important stuff a habit, they can begin to expand their focus to new important stuff. Experienced athletes seem to have mastered all of the important stuff over time—even getting really good at some of the not-so-important stuff. Their experience has built in a greater capacity to know and do more. That was hardly the case when so much was brand-new to them.

It's the same with Anywhere Leaders. When they find themselves in a new role with new expectations and lots of uncertainty, they can easily feel overwhelmed by so many new factors. Feeling quite intimidated at first, they may wonder if they will ever be able to get their arms around the job. In spite of this overwhelmed feeling, however, the Anywhere Leader starts to plug away, starting by keying in on just a few priorities. The Anywhere Leader tells her new formed team, "There's so much to get done. In fact, there's too much. We need to start by identifying the essentials first." Once the essentials are identified, the Anywhere Leader prioritizes them for the organization.

We do the same thing as moms and dads. Last year, a few dads and I took our daughters snowboarding. When we arrived at the airport in Denver, everything was vying for my attention: food, bathroom breaks, baggage claim, ground transportation, and lots of interesting people going in all kinds of directions. I couldn't possibly keep up with all of the inputs my senses were fielding as I raced with my daughter through the terminal. But I had one essential—hang on to my daughter. As long as I had her, everything else would eventually come together. If I lost her, then everything would come to a complete stop.

To grow your perception—your awareness—in uncertain and unfamiliar situations, start by focusing your awareness on the essentials. Ask yourself, *What do I need to listen for the most? Above all else, what is the one thing I need to be evaluating every single day?* By identifying the essentials, you make sure that your perception isn't being diluted by all of the noise clutter that comes with a new assignment.

Recommendation #3: Become More Aware of Your Senses

The speed and complexity of business forces leaders to do more work, faster. Over the last decade, the pace of the work world has become barely manageable for even the best of us—having to maintain peak performance at all times, just to keep up. No wonder we quickly burn out and lose interest in our work. No wonder our health takes a hit. Our feeble bodies just aren't capable of redlining for long periods of time. Eventually, we'll sputter out.

The most successful leaders know when they're moving closer to a collapse. They recognize when they've pushed it too far for too long. And when they do, they'll prioritize rest and recovery. They know that trying to keep up with today's pace of work while trying to trudge forward, exhausted and spent, is just not worth it. They'd rather recover fully and then reengage with maximum power and energy. Because they are self-aware, they know when it's time to rest and recover and when it's time to push themselves hard.

These leaders are dedicated to the work. But they aren't sold out to it. A sold-out leader has sacrificed everything to get ahead—family, health, a sense of purpose, and fun. Such a leader starts her career off in the fast lane, getting promotion after promotion. I've known some of these leaders, and I've been accused of being one at times—it's something I have to watch out for. They start strong, but ten or fifteen years into their career—or less—they've crashed physically, emotionally, even professionally.

Anywhere Leaders are dedicated to their work. But they're also dedicated to life beyond work. While their work is a significant part of their life, they don't want it being the thing that everything else crumbles under.

The question is: How can Anywhere Leaders be so dedicated to their work, making significant sacrifices for the sake of progress, but know full well when it's time to "turn it off" and recover? As I mentioned in Chapter Six, these leaders monitor their own personal key performance indicators (KPIs) that alert them when their lives start to become unhealthy and irresponsible. But Anywhere Leaders are also highly attuned people. They can recognize this in themselves fairly easily. They know they've pushed too hard when they are quicker to anger. They know they've pushed too hard when they come home with no energy for four weeks straight. They see it when they're more easily susceptible to illness. When they see it, they quickly do what's needed to recover.

For this chapter, what's most relevant is what they do about it when they begin to reach the point of exhaustion. Do they just sleep? Is it enough to just slow down the pace? Maybe. But I don't believe that recovery has to be so passive and lethargic, all of the time. Anywhere Leaders use recovery time to grow personally and to expand more of their experiences. They read more things— usually not their business books, but rather religion, history, poetry, or fiction. They might start up a new hobby like photography or wine tasting. Ever try a two-hour lunch? It's extremely difficult to do unless you're agenda-less, and then it's amazing. Anywhere Leaders in rest-and-recovery mode use the time to reconnect with their senses—taking in every sound, smell, taste, and touch, and giving out very little. I don't want to risk oversimplifying, but maybe simplification is exactly what this section of the chapter calls for.

For the sake of recovery, try heightening your awareness of your senses. People who are more aware of their senses are more perceptive. They see details and hear subtle sounds that others miss. Get more in tune with yourself. By increasing your awareness of your senses, you learn to relax, because your focus forces you to slow down enough to be fully aware of the details you are following. You become more aware of tastes because you chew your food slowly. You don't clock your mile run when you're in recovery mode, because you care more about how the wind feels on your face than you do about breaking the six-minute-mile mark. Try getting lost in an art museum. Can you go blind to others around you because you're looking much more deeply into an interesting oil painting? Pay more attention to your breathing. Smell more deeply. Spend more time in quiet contemplation.

During recovery, take everything in and really limit what you give out. By doing so, you will more fully recharge, and you will grow more attuned to your senses—something that will be very valuable to you as an Anywhere Leader when the pace and uncertainty of work ramps up.

Recommendation #4: Trust Your Perceptions and Follow Your Gut

Do you ever get that feeling where you say to yourself, *I shouldn't be here. Something just doesn't feel right.* Movies often portray these moments with someone walking down a dark alley and then she's suddenly frightened by a black cat knocking over a trashcan. When we find ourselves in those situations—when it's dark, when we aren't too familiar with things around us, or sudden loud sounds surprise us, or we see vague shadows lurking in the fog—our intuition likely tells us to get outta there because there is impending danger. That's your intuition or your gut feeling. More perceptive people have more awareness and are often more intuitive than people with subdued perception.

Your intuition is subconscious and triggers several physiological effects. Your face suddenly turns pale, you get goose bumps all over, and the hair rises on your arm. Why? Because your intuition is your subconscious brain releasing adrenaline to your body so you can defend yourself better or flee quicker. The adrenaline oxygenates the parts of your body that are best equipped to fight or take flight.

Scientists suggest that our intuition is a legitimate subconscious feeling for us to follow when we have no other data available to us. In uncertainty and in unfamiliar situations where no precedent is set, our intuition is really all we have to work from.

Intuition works like this: Our brain has a subconscious component that can recall memories that our conscious mind has completely forgotten about or ignored. Or the memory may be planted so deeply in our mind that recalling it might take a significant amount of time. Our intuition manifests when our subconscious, or unconscious mind, connects past experiences or observations with our current situation in an instant. Our subconscious mind seems to bypass any logical sequence, thereby rapidly delivering important messages through feelings to our bodies. When you don't have time to logically mine your memories for related experiences, your subconscious brain decides to take over.

Intuition or gut feeling is a very accurate feeling that is subconsciously logical. As leaders, we should follow it when a critical decision is needed faster than we can consciously and methodically analyze it. Remember Jim Burke in Chapter Two? He used a lot of gut instinct and intuition when making some huge decisions following the Tylenol crisis. People wanted to know what Tylenol maker Johnson & Johnson was going to do about the bottle tampering, before Burke and his leadership team had enough time to really consider their actions. I'm sure his conscious and subconscious minds were both hard at work—with his conscious mind questioning some of his moves. America wanted and deserved immediate answers when there was no time to really contemplate them.

We should follow our gut instincts when we have very little information available yet a decision is necessary. I recall the comments from a past chess champion, Gary Kasparov, to be a little surprising. I had always thought of chess champions to be the most methodical and logical thinkers. But Kasparov, who claims to be able to think fifteen moves ahead, said he could never think of every logical move and its resulting impact. There's not enough time to capture and analyze all of the information, the possibilities, and predict the outcome. Even Kasparov uses a significant amount of intuition and claims that "intuition is a defining quality of a great chess player."

Anywhere Leaders use their intuition when they have no precedent for a given situation they face. And because Anywhere Leaders operate in uncertainty, they are often operating with no precedent to follow. For much of the Anywhere Leader's work, the book isn't written. That's when intuition should step in.

Unbridled intuition can deliver some pretty extensive consequences, however, so the Anywhere Leader is careful. Following the terrorist attacks of September 11, 2001, many more people were told by their subconscious mind not to fly anymore because it was just too dangerous. With fewer people traveling on airplanes, highway traffic went up. In the year after the attacks, logically highway fatalities significantly increased, while no fatalities occurred on commercial passenger air travel.

Anywhere Leaders know how to balance their intuition and logical thinking. When the data are available and there is time to mine the data to get to a smart and logical decision, Anywhere Leaders rely on the data. When logic and rationale exist, they depend more on those resources than on their intuition.

When an Anywhere Leader is emotionally connected to something, she keeps her intuition in check. She realizes that her emotions can override a smart decision and fuel her intuition if she's not careful. Anywhere Leaders intentionally seek out more logic and rationale when they find themselves emotionally connected to a decision.

But as life becomes more unstructured and more unpredictable, we will likely need to let our intuition play a stronger role in decision making. Anywhere Leaders don't hesitate to rely on their intuition during times of uncertainty and unpredictability.

As you consider growing your perception as an Anywhere Leader, follow the recommendations of this chapter:

- Become a continuous learner. Be eager to take on new and challenging assignments that help you grow your knowledge and increase your awareness. Tap into more resources to increase your knowledge inputs.

- Focus on being keenly aware of the essentials to fend off the noise clutter. Identify that one thing that you need to be monitoring every single day.

- Get more in tune with yourself by growing more aware of your senses during times of rest and recovery so that you can leverage them for peak performance. To become more aware of your senses, take time to take in more and limit what you give out.

- Trust your perceptions. Embrace your intuition when the data doesn't exist and follow your gut when decisions are necessary in uncertain and unpredictable circumstances.

Part Four

VASTLY RESOURCEFUL

11

DOING A LOT WITH A LITTLE HELPS THE ANYWHERE LEADER SUCCEED

U p to this point, you've probably pictured the Anywhere Leader as a polished professional in a pressed suit with great shoes and a leather laptop bag. Or maybe it's more casual: nice jeans, great shoes, and a canvas messenger bag. But you probably didn't envision Tom Hanks in a loincloth with a beard down to his chest and a chewed-up volleyball for a friend. Yet his character in the Robert Zemeckis film *Castaway*, FedEx exec Chuck Noland, was the ultimate Anywhere Leader.

That's how he wound up on a deserted island in the first place. As a systems engineer, Noland flew around the world, trouble-shooting and solving problems wherever he landed—including, as it turned out, in the middle of the Pacific Ocean when his plane crashed. Talk about resourceful: this guy took a sheet of plastic from a portable toilet that washed up and turned it into a sail for a makeshift raft. He learned how to spear fish and build fires without matches. But if his plane had not crashed and he had made it to his destination, he no doubt would have been equally creative in solving whatever crisis awaited him there.

Like Noland, Anywhere Leaders can find themselves in some fairly sparse environments. They're often the ones put on the "yet to be baked" and unresourced assignments because they have proven to be resourceful, finding ways to do a lot with a little. The strengths behind their resourcefulness are *imaginative*, *inclusive*, and *inventive*—Anywhere Leaders are all three. They understand that whenever there's a transition, the resources they once had may disappear. Yet these leaders are able to effectively plan using whatever tools, material, and talent they have access to.

Resourcefulness is born out of necessity—a point that became profoundly clear to me the night I ran across a tiny man in a dark alley in Deep Ellum, an eclectic neighborhood in Dallas. Robert Hines was homeless and desperate. He saw me park my car behind a building on my way to a dinner at a nearby restaurant. Deep Ellum had lots of homeless people living on its streets, so it wasn't unusual to be approached for a handout. When Mr. Hines approached me in the dark, I quickly discounted him and tried to ignore him by keeping my head down and picking up my walking pace. When he was able to stop me and ask for money, I hurriedly fumbled through my wallet and realized I had only a few twenties— and I didn't want to turn them over to a total stranger in some back alley.

I did, however, explain to Mr. Hines that if he was still around when I left the restaurant, I'd give him some of the change from my dinner. As I continued to walk away, he was persistent, giving me some pretty creative reasons for why I should give up the money.

The situation reminded me of a formula I once read:

Necessity + Creativity + Persistence = Resourcefulness

Robert Hines had desperate needs (necessity). He showed remarkable persistence. And I was about to learn how creative he was.

Before I could run off, Hines reached down into his roughed up backpack and pulled out the rattiest homemade booklet. The front and back covers were made of pink construction paper, badly stained with dirt and spilled drinks. The binding was duct tape. Hines handed me the book and told me that he had written it— over eighty pages of poems, by Robert Hines, The Deep Ellum Poet. I flipped through this little book of poems and was immediately impressed. So I discounted him again. "Mr. Hines," I said. "You didn't write this. C'mon." He said, "Sure I did. My favorite one is on page fourteen." As I started turning to page fourteen, he began to recite it from memory—with amazing passion.

I was completely humbled and even taken aback. This guy with no food and no place to sleep lived with more inspiration that I did—and I had everything I could ever need or want.

I bought his book for twenty bucks. I've read it cover to cover a few times, and it is brilliant. Hines wasn't only persistent, he was creative—developing a craft with hardly a resource, and asking people to buy his creative works. I never saw him again, but he has deeply impacted my life by his humility, his perseverance, and his ability to remain passionate and inspired through the toughest of circumstances. Robert Hines taught me that the gap between my life and his just isn't that big. He made a few bad decisions that cost him everything—his family, his comfort, and his career.

But here's where the story gets pretty amazing. A few years later, a friend of mine whom I had shared this story with forwarded me an article from a Dallas newspaper that featured Robert Hines. I expected the story to be tragic. Far from it. This story featured Robert Hines's work of poetry. Mr. Hines, the Deep Ellum Poet, is published, and has received a number of honors. His book, now with a legit cover, is available in many different outlets, including Amazon.com.

Robert Hines had nothing. No money. No home. No possibilities. He had to use every tiny and insignificant scrap in life to get by. But his use of those morsels—stained construction paper, heavily abused backpack, duct tape, and begging—helped him to achieve the extraordinary. I encourage you to buy his book. You can be inspired, too.

When we live with abundance, there's little need for resourcefulness. Instead, we create a lot of waste. Every meal is new; throw away the leftovers. Our leadership is often the same way. But Anywhere Leaders emulate Robert Hines in their own work.

Take Inventory and Anticipate Change

In tough times, the Anywhere Leader looks at what she has and asks, *What are all the things I can create with this set of materials? What can I do with limits?* And she's an innovative thinker in good times, too. The Anywhere Leader is as resourceful with abundance as she is with scarcity, constantly looking for ways to do more with more. Even with a wealth of resources, she examines situations from all angles. She still explores the many possibilities, solutions, and things she can make with what she has. The Anywhere Leader is constantly taking inventory, striving to stay ahead of the situation by being keenly aware of everything that is available, even when she doesn't necessarily need it.

Resourceful leaders are always planning for the "what ifs"—anticipating potential shifts, disruptions, and changes. Anticipation helps them adapt to shifts—or to harmonize with change. Keep that word "harmonize" in mind; I'll have more to say about it soon.

Taking inventory and anticipating change are essential behaviors for resourceful leaders. I learned this lesson the hard way when I had my own Chuck Noland experience, sailing off of Puerto Rico. The adventure side of me wanted to check off the box of sailing in the Bermuda Triangle. It wasn't a long outing, just over half of a day. The sail out of Puerto Rico was perfect—beautiful day, fairly light winds, and reasonably calm waters. That meant I could sit back, relax, and enjoy the ride. My mistake was expecting the same conditions on my return. But the early weather report I got that morning was way off, and I didn't anticipate anything other than smooth sailing both ways. As I made my turn to head back to Puerto Rico, the skies darkened and the winds shifted and picked up significantly. My pretty straight shot back to the dock would now have to be full of tacking maneuvers (ninety-degree turns to catch the wind). My planned four-hour sail was likely going to take more than six hours—that meant sailing in the dark in an unfamiliar location, with the seas getting much rougher. I got my adventure.

Darkness came and the island disappeared. Thankfully it wasn't stormy. The waves were the biggest I had experienced, and now I had to navigate them with no visibility. I hadn't precisely charted my course before getting into this mess, nor had I become familiar with the northeast corner of Puerto Rico, so I was truly returning blind. With most of my navigational tools in the cabin of the boat, making a dash for them by leaving the helm in rough waters was going to be too risky. I chose to rely on my compass and a lighthouse in the distance that I knew was on the tip of Fajardo, Puerto Rico. If I could keep that lighthouse ten degrees off the starboard side of my bow, I'd be really close to staying on course. I'd have to assume that there were no obstacles between the lighthouse and me, and that the lighthouse was fairly close to the edge of the shore. It was a gamble that I hadn't anticipated having to take. Fortunately, I didn't hit anything on my way in. Once I passed the lighthouse safely, I recognized the city lights of Fajardo and could ride the shoreline back to the dock.

Two and half hours later I docked with a torn sail from the fierce winds. I was dog tired and soaking wet from the splash. What had started off as a fun sail became quite a tiring challenge for which I was ill prepared. If I had anticipated better, I could have been much more prepared, with adequate navigational tools, a better plan, and a shorter sail.

Resourceful leaders are rarely caught in such circumstances. But when they are, they're prepared, not surprised. They know how to quickly assess and sift through a lot of information and quickly put together a workable solution.

Allow Artistry in Your Leadership

Resourceful leaders seem to be one part engineer and one part artist—meaning that they can effectively act on their imagination. They can envision a solution— what to put on that blank canvas— and then get to work. As author Daniel Pink describes it so eloquently, resourceful leaders have the ability to orchestrate a "symphony."

We've highlighted a couple of words—*harmonize* and *symphony*— that are atypical of a business leadership book. As we think about today's most successful leaders, we will find connections with concepts and qualities not commonly associated with leadership. After all, there's a great amount of artistry involved in running a business or a division, or in leading a team. Why? Because artists stimulate our emotions, and so should the most effective leaders. Artists use their imagination, creativity, and skill to ignite our passions and force our reactions. Symphony conductors make us forget that beneath the beautiful ensemble is a brilliant combination of individual voices and instruments. Effective leaders are like these conductors, as they resource the right individuals into a collective charge toward a compelling mission. Because of their ability to envision the ensemble before a single note is played and their ability to put the right people in place to make it happen, it's no wonder that they have significant influence on their employees.

They're also able to create some really cool product ideas that connect with consumers or customers.

Use Your Imagination and Be Inclusive

Many claim that entrepreneur Richard Branson's most significant value comes from his ability to dream up stuff and then put organizational capacity behind it. Branson, the founder of Virgin, is a consummate daydreamer. (My kind of guy. I spent many afternoons in detention for daydreaming in school.) The point is that there are many extraordinary thinkers who break the mold of what often passes for good leadership. Today's leaders must be able to imagine new worlds of possibilities. Mark Zuckerberg did when he founded Facebook. Howard Schultz, founder of Starbucks, did the same when he envisioned a café-style restaurant business model that dared to bring respectability and professionalism to a customer service job that Americans usually considered "low class"—the behind-the-counter coffeehouse barista. Schultz did a lot of imagining. The *New York Times*, in an interview with Schultz, pointed out that his imagination was running wild one day as he was sitting at one of Milan's many espresso bars. He saw that the coffee shops in Milan were an integral part of social life for Italians. Schultz then asked himself, *Why not Seattle?*

Herb Kelleher did a lot of imagining for Southwest Airlines and encouraged an imaginative, spirited, and creative culture. Kelleher's challenge was not in enabling such a culture, but rather in keeping Southwest's culture from being too defined by the people who wanted to limit imagination and create acronyms to circumvent creativity. Once Southwest began to experience rapid growth, many of its leaders developed the mindset, "This is how it's done. Let's capture it, slap a formula on it, develop the Southwest language, and institutionalize our operations and processes." If Kelleher had allowed that way of thinking to drive its strategy, then Southwest might look like a lot of those other struggling airlines. Instead, the Southwest culture empowers its employees and their imaginative ideas. At Southwest, the creative, inclusive, and fun culture is king. Want an example? Get on YouTube.com and search for "David Holmes, Southwest's Flight Attendant Rapper." He raps his announcements before every flight. Southwest loves it and invited him to take the stage at one of its major conferences. Other airlines might have written him up for breaking policy.

Kelleher saw the value of imagination and openness at every level within the organization. So does Steve Jobs. Jobs didn't think up the design of the iPod. Rank and file contractor Tony Fadell did. Fadell pushed his idea through design and engineering before even presenting the idea to top management at Apple. These imaginative leaders, no matter their level, ignite their organizations with their creative spark. Imagination is right-brained stuff. The Anywhere Leader taps the power of the right brain.

Leaders who can imagine are leaders who don't get stuck. When cornered, they can quickly think up an escape. Because of their imaginative abilities, Anywhere Leaders are often behind some pretty cool turnaround stories. Such stories abound—before Amazon.com became profitable, it was often referred to as Amazon .bomb. Naysayers came out in droves proclaiming that this highly cash-leveraged company would never sail, but would be another venture capitalist money pit. To them, the bust of the technology bubble spelled doom for this Internet economy poster child. You may recall that earlier in the book I presented Amazon CEO Jeff Bezos as an example. He was a creative leader who kept imagining solutions and generating valuable ideas that ignited Amazon's charge. While others looked at the Internet economy as an online storefront for transactions, Bezos saw the need to build a community of active and like-minded consumers to achieve scale. His imagination allowed him to envision a different business model for retail and to pursue different strategies that hadn't been considered before. Significant changes and adjustments have always been demanded of Amazon. The company's ability to adapt, or harmonize, with its opportunities started with its ability to imagine a way out of some pretty dark corners.

Imagination, as Bezos could no doubt tell you, is fueled by ideas. Ideas are generated by people. And people are shaped by their experiences. More collective experiences equal more collective ideas, which means greater imagination to create, solve, and build. Anywhere Leaders know that their most valuable resource is people, which is why they are highly inclusive in their leadership. Inclusiveness is one of the most critical concepts in business, and one of the most twisted and misunderstood, as well. The term has been tied intrinsically to corporate initiatives aimed at creating a more racially, ethnically, and culturally diverse workplace. Nothing wrong with that! A diverse workplace is the best possible setting for resourceful leaders in today's worldwide business environment.

Where the concept gets twisted is when leaders confuse inclusiveness with like-mindedness—and ideas with ideals. People don't need to hold the same views in order to share their perspectives and listen to the perspectives of others. They just need to work in an environment that fosters openness and accepts *disagreement* in order for ideas to flow freely. In some cases, corporate diversity initiatives have gone to such extremes to promote consensus and cooperation that they've done the exact opposite: they've created a climate of defensiveness and distrust. By trying to institutionalize openness, they've actually closed off people. (But that's a topic for another book.)

The issues surrounding diversity programs are sensitive and most companies are still feeling their way around them. But for the Anywhere Leader, being inclusive is not an initiative; it's an imperative. It has nothing to do with corporate agendas. Anywhere Leaders know that being open to views that are different from— and even opposed to—their own is the only way to gather the best ideas and harness the greatest talent. If you shut out different perspectives, you lose one of your most valuable resources: people and their ideas. If you're defensive of your own positions, you create a bunker mentality whereby nobody, including yourself, shares anything of value with anyone else.

Anywhere Leaders don't rush to judgment of someone else's ideas or ideals, because they are strong in their own convictions, yet interested in differing viewpoints. They understand that you don't have to deny your own beliefs or background in order to consider and appreciate those of others. They're not afraid of dialogue or debate; in fact, they encourage it, because they know that inclusion is not agreement or consensus—rather, inclusion is involvement.

One of my favorite people is a woman I used to work with named Kasey Loman. She is a creative genius, incredibly smart, and amazingly fast in her work. When we worked together, I went to her with important projects and sought her advice. Outside of the office, I enjoyed her company. She is very interesting to me, and a good friend. She also brews her own really good beer. She is gay and I'm not. Our political views are often at odds—although not as much as some might think. At times, we've even debated a couple of our political positions, never coming to agreement. But our disagreement never gets in the way of our involvement, because we both find our relationship to be rewarding and enriching. We appreciate each other, so there's never a need to be at odds or to build protective bunkers.

While this book isn't focused on diversity, I can't overemphasize the importance of inclusion for the sake of involvement. Anywhere Leaders succeed in any environment because they are open to influence from everywhere. They aren't intimidated by the differences or dissenting positions of others, because they are enlightened and self-aware. The paradox is that they are confident in their positions, yet open to influence. Managing this paradox as an Anywhere Leader comes down to establishing a set of principles in your life that apply no matter what the circumstance or situation may be—but not making *everything* in your life a nonnegotiable.

Leaders who don't manage that paradox end up being the "my way or the highway" guys. They're the real know-it-alls who have staunch opinions about everything. Nothing short of a real life crisis will move them from their position. In a recent review of the history of leadership in the *Consulting Psychology Journal: Practice and Research*, prominent management researcher Gary

Yukl and colleague Rubina Mahsud reinforced this notion: Leaders who dig in and who fail to change or adapt are less than they could be. It gets worse when they view themselves as organizational saviors who have been brought in to "right the ship." But more often than not, they end up sinking it. Why? Usually, because these leaders unintentionally become culture killers.

There are many examples of company founders and chief executives who have inspired their organization with their humility, drive, and ability to connect emotionally with others. Sam Walton was often photographed on one knee in a Walmart shopping aisle talking with, and not to, Walmart associates. But the examples of emotionally connected and inclusive leaders don't seem to always get through to executive boards working on the succession plan for their CEO. Good companies with good leaders nevertheless somehow work the "my way or the highway" leader into their succession plans. To fantasize an outlandish example, let's imagine Tony Hsieh, CEO of the highly successful and culturally thriving retailer Zappos.com, being succeeded by someone like North Korea's Kim Jong Il. You can imagine the succession committee justifying their choice: *Sure, Kim Jong Il is a tyrant, but despite the threats and sanctions, North Korea is getting by.* Perhaps this comparison is bizarre—but companies do follow a similar process for their top succession plans. The typical story goes like this: Engaging, visionary founder and CEO can really connect, inspire, and ignite a culture. In response to his upcoming retirement, the board searches for his successor—likely outside of the company. The board views this as an opportunity to elevate the firm's "operational savvy." Out goes Hseih, in comes Jong Il. A full-on attack aimed at the inclusive culture is launched, and within a few short months or years, everyone wonders why the implementation of operational best practices isn't having quite the impact that investors had expected.

Not so outlandish is the real succession story of Gateway founder Ted Waitt, who handpicked AT&T executive Jeff Weitzen to succeed him in the year 2000. Weitzen was a rigid, micromanaging policymaker and the culture killer for Gateway. This was a complete style shift from Waitt's easygoing office demeanor. One year later, Waitt was back at the helm. Past IBM CEO Lou Gerstner once said, "Culture is everything." For Gerstner, Waitt, and other imaginative, inclusive, and inspiring leaders, culture isn't "a" thing, it's "the" thing.

As an Anywhere Leader, your culture has to be about inclusion, which means it's never "your way or the highway." But remember the paradox—being a leader of an inclusive culture doesn't mean you have agreement or consensus across the board. You will need to manage your ability to listen and be influenced, but you will also be forced to decide. Inclusion doesn't take away your decision-making power. The hope is that it helps you make better decisions. "Your way" may be right. But you're not going to send people to the "highway" for their dissenting opinion.

So how does the Anywhere Leader concept of inclusion play in to being resourceful? Well, the very definition of inclusion is "addition." Being inclusive of others helps you build trusted relationships. Having trusted relationships lets you engage other people—involving them, calling on them more, asking more of them, and adding to your capacity and capability. When I started my business career in sales, one of my first purchases was the 3x5 Rolodex rotary card file. I quickly learned in 1992 that it was important to have a big Rolodex—the bigger the card file, the more bragging rights, and the more successful you were at sales. It was important to bulk up that thing with all kinds of names and phone numbers. After all, success was about building your network. A few years later, you could import your Rolodex digitally into your phone. The bigger your phone list, the more successful you were in sales. Because of this need to build the ultimate list of contacts, I'd grab a card from anyone at any time. I'd go to dinners to glad-hand whenever possible. And even though I tilt toward introversion, I viewed this networking thing as my job. But such approaches were rarely productive. Today, having a lot of contacts may be somewhat valuable—but it's more valuable to have a number of people whom you can depend on and whom you can leverage. I had hundreds of names in my Rolodex. However, I may have been able to depend on only about 5 percent of those contacts.

I still see this behavior in so many leaders today—growing their contact lists merely for the sake of volume. While they may be expanding their network, they aren't building valuable relationships. Valuable relationships don't happen by chance meetings or at glad-handing social events with an exchange of contact information. Valuable relationships are developed through mutual investment. I can go to lots of dinner socials and meet some really nice people. But I can't use them when I need them. I can continue to build my following on Twitter, but my request for a major favor in the Twitterverse will surely be ignored.

The Anywhere Leader doesn't just build casual relationships through networking; rather, she invests significantly in those relationships that are valuable to her. She goes beyond the social events and the contact information exchange, spending real time learning about the other person, sharing more deeply with the person, and being more open with her discussion. But the Anywhere Leader doesn't just invest in those relationships that are most comfortable, either. She wants diverse relationships. She wants to learn from others who are different from her. And she wants their relationships to be additional or inclusive in value—gaining more insight and new perspectives.

When Anywhere Leaders build inclusive relationships, they are better able to use them broadly across their business. They have brokered relationships that are vastly applicable across any number of needs. I may not be Latino, but I have several relationships with people who are; among other benefits, I can use them to help me to understand the buying habits of Latino consumers.

In my business, academicians are elevated for their knowledge. They are the research experts, and their knowledge is accessed worldwide. I'm not an academician. My education goes only through a master's degree. But when I need to validate the findings behind our research, I call upon any number of academics who can help with that process. And they rely on me. While these academics are immersed in research, my team and I at SVI are immersed in real live business cases and scenarios. When I come together with my researcher friends, academia meets business application.

The point is, I could surround myself with people just like me, but my lack of inclusion would limit my impact. Inclusion is addition, and Anywhere Leaders love addition. When they are assigned to a start-up, they make new start-up friends. When they are elevated to the C-suite, they add C-suite connections. When they are deployed abroad, they develop in-country friends. And while developing all of these new relationships, they stay close to some of those older and deeper relationships as well. They are prepared for anything, because they are resourceful with a broad relationship base of diverse talent that they've invested heavily in developing.

Broad and diverse relationships across and beyond your company enable you to tackle some pretty crazy requests—and obtain good outcomes. The best outcomes happen when you have a culture of co-creators, cooperators, and contributors. They occur when you use your entire company for the best ideas. When others draw back, the Anywhere Leader inquires. Her best leadership comes from her ability to create an inclusive culture that maximizes the impact of every single individual in her organization, not from her ability to think up a good idea. In fact, the Anywhere Leader loves the collective idea-generating process just as much as the big idea itself. We see this approach more and more in the marketplace through crowd-sourcing and user-generated content, where anyone can participate and create, and lots and lots of people do. Why don't our leaders embrace the same idea? Involve many—make better, move faster.

Don't Just Dream It—Invent It

When a leader uses his broad resources and puts them behind imaginative ideas, invention is born. That's what invention is: action behind imagination. Take away the action, and you've got a whole lot of creative people with a thousand great ideas that never see the light of day. Anywhere Leaders put ideas into action. They don't imagine with their eyes closed; rather, they are constantly looking for the "how to" part of the idea. They are the stargazers with tools in hand, ready to start hammering on their rocket ship. Richard Branson of Virgin is one. He didn't just dream of cheaper space travel. He built a spaceship—two of them, actually—appropriately named SpaceShipOne and SpaceShipTwo. Martin Luther King Jr. didn't just deliver a speech; he created a movement and led the charge for civil rights that changed the world. Remember Doc Brown, the crazy inventor in the movie *Back to the Future* who turned the DeLorean into a time machine? He always had his laboratory coat on. He was always tinkering.

That's why Anywhere Leaders aren't dreamers. They are inventors who tinker in laboratories with other inventors, who test ideas, and who sometimes hammer away on things just to see if they can get something to work. Sounds a little risky, huh? Well, it is. Anywhere Leaders are sometimes behind some accidental explosions. Like the Wright Brothers, they've crashed their share of airplanes. Like Thomas Edison, they've found one thousand ways not to invent an incandescent light bulb. But no matter what, their attempts are always for progress. When others get stuck, the Anywhere Leader moves. When solutions don't exist, he creates one. An overused but a perfect illustration is the story of the imperiled *Apollo 13* space mission to the moon, commanded by Captain Jim Lovell. During its flight toward the moon, one of the spacecraft's oxygen tanks ruptured, severely damaging the spacecraft's electrical system.

It was a terrifying day for NASA's space program, as a safe return home for the astronauts was in question. Everyone involved, from the flight crew to mission control, had to get inventive real fast. If you've seen the eponymous movie, then you may recall the scene where NASA employees got into a room to solve a carbon dioxide gas exposure problem. The astronauts were breathing bad air while they were trying to stay alive in the lunar module, which wasn't equipped to provide oxygen and sustain life for a long length of time. The crew and mission control had to take whatever they had available from the command module and create clean oxygen cartridges for the lunar module. The scene shows several mission control workers in a room throwing out every command module item onto a big table to see what they can use to invent oxygen cartridges that create clean, breathable air.

Like the crew of *Apollo 13*, Anywhere Leaders often find themselves in situations where there is no field guide and no instruction manual. They've got to be keen observers of what's available. They have to assess their resources, get creative with them, organize them into something workable, and put them to work—fast. With every step, inventive leaders question existing modes and create new ones. They are consummate learners who want to understand the bigger, broader picture and all of its implications. They're not satisfied with gaining two or three new insights—they want *every* available insight at their fingertips to put to good use. Inventive leaders don't fear people who are smarter than they are, or who know more than they do on a given topic, or who fundamentally disagree with them. They embrace such people. They want them all in the room. The work is all about the idea, not about them. People buy the inventions, not the inventors.

These inventive Anywhere Leaders have a keen eye for vestigial, linear-style, reactionary thinking—and they often quickly winnow it out. As resourceful leaders, they don't think individual stars; they think constellations, universes. They don't just worry about an illness; they are concerned about total wellness, too.

Simply solving the problem is not their goal. Their aim is to deliver remedies that either eliminate the source of the problem or change the environment that allowed the problem to emerge.

Michelle is an Anywhere Leader, and a very successful fashion designer. She started her career in the fashion district in Los Angeles. Everything was available to her there—the materials, the models, the reviewers, the sales reps, and the retailers. She had mastered her job and built strong relationships that helped sell her designs to top retailers. But Michelle was ready for her next challenge, and her company sent her overseas to work on a new line of swimsuits. She had hoped for Milan, London, or Paris, but this work took her to Hong Kong. Because this was a new swimsuit line, she didn't expect a large staff with lots of support—and she was right. Where were the fabrics and materials, the seamstresses and textile manufacturers? Michelle realized that she was going to have to start from scratch, leading a few employees who barely spoke her language and were very green in the fashion business.

Michelle started by trying to build the Los Angeles business model in Hong Kong. She tried to build the relationships and bring the necessary resources in-house. But the low experience level of fashion designers and fashion workers in Hong Kong quickly began to impact the quality of the fashion line. Michelle was also noticing that her team was missing her deadlines—a major problem in the seasonal fashion business. Michelle was going to have to rethink her entire business model to salvage her work.

She stopped looking at what was wrong with Hong Kong and started to consider what was right. Hong Kong would never be LA. But Hong Kong could be better in a lot of ways. After all, it offered more connections and a global network. Hong Kong was light years ahead of Los Angeles in worldwide supply chain management practices. Michelle didn't have much experience in LA with supply chain management, but she quickly realized the value of third-party sourcing in Hong Kong. She could analyze the trends and then invent the process for third-party sourcing.

Her small office stayed small. Her team focused on trend research, design sketches, third-party manufacturing, and fashion brokerage. By evaluating their available resources and reinventing their business model, they were able to improve their quality, meet their deadlines, and increase their profits. Michelle fought against linear, dogmatic thinking, observed all that was available to her, pieced it together, and put it to work successfully—and quite differently from how it was done in Los Angeles.

Anywhere Leaders who succeed in a crisis situation or unknown territory—whether it's Hong Kong or outer space—are, by definition, resourceful. They're resourceful because they allow themselves the freedom to imagine. They involve other people, especially those with perspectives different from their own. And they put ideas into action.

So how do you develop your ability to be resourceful, other than asking yourself *WWMD?* (*What would MacGyver do?*) Let's start with learning how to become more imaginative.

12

BECOME IMAGINATIVE

If you find yourself in an interview for a new job and the interviewer asks you what you think your greatest strength is, don't answer, "My imagination." The likely response will be "OK. Let's see—nope. I have no other questions for you. Thank you for your time. I'll call you if I need you." And that's the last you'll ever hear from the prospective employer.

If creative leaders are said to be so valuable to our businesses, then why do we fear the imagination of our workers? After all, the imagination is the creative faculty of the mind. We need creative thinkers, and creative thinking requires imagination. Maybe one of the reasons that imagination hasn't been so valued in business settings or in academia is because imagination is often associated with fantasy—and who wants a bunch of leaders who are all caught up in fantasy?

So what's the difference? Fantasies are of myths and legends. Fantasy is opposed to reason. Fantasy is idle. Imagination, on the other hand, takes effort and considers reason. We can fall asleep in fantasy, but our imagination forces us to stay awake and remain engaged. Like fantasy, however, imagination doesn't operate within boundaries. Imagination isn't dependent on perceived reality. Albert Einstein said, "Imagination . . . is more important than knowledge. Knowledge is limited. Imagination encircles the world."

When unimaginative leaders are in charge, companies can grow stale. These leaders don't like to change their processes or make organizational adjustments, because they cannot envision anything other than what already exists. As long as things go as planned, unimaginative leaders can be successful. But when markets and consumer demands change, these leaders have a hard time remaining relevant. Anywhere Leaders are highly imaginative and able to help keep their companies relevant when the business landscape changes, and they are able to solve difficult problems through their creativity.

So how does one become more imaginative?

Recommendation #1: Don't Channel Your Mental Energy—Unleash It

Recently I delivered a presentation to a group on the topic of emotional intelligence. After I was done writing the presentation, I realized how uninteresting it was. The presentation was overly academic and packed with heavy research. The science and research behind emotional intelligence was important, for sure, but the presentation had no flavor. And I needed to make the research and the topic applicable to the audience. So I started to consider real-life examples of emotional intelligence that I could reference. Several examples came to mind, but none of them were compelling. I was stuck with no compelling example to bring the application to life, until I finally freed my thinking. Instead of trying to think of an emotional intelligence example, I started to consider examples that would just be plain interesting—adding flavor to the presentation. Without limiting my brain to consider only those experiences or examples with a direct emotional intelligence link, I'd have a much more expansive library of examples to draw from. I could think of the most interesting stories first and then see if somehow, some way, they could tie to the topic. Tying a compelling story to the topic was much easier for me than trying to identify an example through the topic's narrow channel.

That's a practice I try to take with every presentation I deliver. When I give a talk or write a scenario to back up a point I'm trying to make, I don't go through my mental Rolodex in search of an anecdote or analogy that fits. I go through my mental Rolodex looking for my most intriguing or interesting experiences—and then I see if it somehow supports my point. I focus on what's interesting first, and then what's applicable—not the other way around. Right brain first, then left brain.

Disney gets it. There's a term that Disney has popularized, "imagineering," which describes the team responsible for designing and developing its theme parks. The word itself suggests the proper order—first *imagine*, then *engineer*. The team wants to know whether an idea is "magical" before they start working on the blueprints.

So should you. Begin your imaginative session with as few boundaries as possible. Be careful not to go too quickly to the limitations of the details before you capture the magic. Once you've imagined up a compelling idea or example, then by all means, engage the left brain—put structure to it and make it work.

The next time you're tapping the creative mind, and compelling examples are failing to materialize, ask yourself, *When I'm brainstorming, do I start by establishing all of the boundaries and limitations in my head, or do I start processing my ideas with a blank canvas? Am I allowing my right brain the freedom of letting my thoughts flow, or do I start by engaging my left brain, putting the analytical side before the creative side?*

Anywhere Leaders are imaginative: they give their right brain the opportunity to span far and wide before they begin to whittle the idea into something workable.

Recommendation #2: Consider Reason as You Imagine

Don't worry, left brainers. This recommendation is for you. Your left brain plays a role in imagination by introducing reason—not as a limitation, but as a consideration. Your left brain keeps your creative thinking targeted and far from fantasy. Our imagination has a target. We imagine for a purpose or a point. Having a target for our imagination helps our imagination stay reasonable and productive. The Wright Brothers used their imagination to envision flight. Flight was their target. And their imagination ran wild (a good thing) trying to build a glider that could sustain flight. They took what they learned from making bicycles and imagined those mechanics at work in a flying machine. If the Wright Brothers had fantasized about flight, they may have had visions of levitation instead. Levitation would be unreasonable, bizarre, and unproductive.

We use our imagination to envision a new solution to a problem and to think up stories that would help us communicate our points better. Imagineers are behind new product designs. Their imagination inspires company cultures because they create compelling organizational visions. Imaginative leaders are behind organizational restructures; they see new opportunities to which others are completely oblivious. And in all of those cases, imagination has a target—to get better, to improve, to progress, and to win. And to do those things, you can't allow your imagination to spin off into fantasy.

As you imagine, you're not worried about the level of difficulty of your idea—most newly imagined ideas are difficult. As you imagine, you need not let yourself be limited by existing barriers.

Your imagination should, however, remain reasonable and productive. Therefore, as you imagine, you should consider these questions: Does the idea have a target or an objective (not random and irrelevant), and is this idea possible? If it's possible and relevant, then your imagination is likely productive.

Recommendation #3: Don't Wait for It—Work for It

I can imagine that some of you may be dismissing this right-brained talk because you just aren't wired that way. For you, this creative idea stuff is just not cool or comfortable. You want the process because you're a process worker—and you're good at it. Define something, and you can systematically figure your way through it with the best of 'em. But I believe that there's a significant misconception about right-brained thinkers. The misconception is that creative thinkers can simply sit back and let their mind wonder until the "Aha!" hits, that they're just waiting for inspiration to strike. The misconception might even paint the picture of a creative genius who is somewhat socially inept, but wants to be in touch and in tune with his inner world—even zoning out at times.

When I think of true creative geniuses, people like Stephen King and Steven Spielberg come to mind. And when I read about people like them, I learn quickly just how much work they put into their creative craft. Creativity for them doesn't just happen. It takes a whole lot of discipline. King, in his book *On Writing*, said that people who want to be good writers should write every single day. He does—even when he doesn't feel like it. Like you, like all of us, Stephen King doesn't feel creative and inspired all the time. He works at it. The creative process is like mining. You've got to dig through a lot of rock before you get to the precious metal. Jack London, the American author and activist, famously said: "You can't wait for inspiration. You have to go after it with a club."

How much discipline are you putting into your creative thinking? Do you write on the days that you don't really feel like writing? Do you make time to work your creative right brain, or do you let it slide because "it's just not you"?

Anywhere Leaders don't wait for their muse to appear. They carve out the time to exercise their creative minds almost every day through reading or writing, singing or painting, designing or whatever else might come to mind. So should you. Put your right brain to work. Your creativity will grow if you exercise it.

Recommendation #4: Don't Settle—Find Your Setting

Sometimes there just doesn't seem to be time for such exercising of your imaginative mind. If your inner artist decided to hit the road after kindergarten, then creative imagination may not be a high priority for you. Other things can easily occupy your mind— profit and loss statements, Microsoft project plans, that complex Excel spreadsheet full of data. For you, it may be necessary to intentionally carve out specific time and a specific place for your imagination and creativity to flow. Stephen King has a place where he goes to escape the noise of the world; a place where, as he describes it, he can begin to dream.

Tim Harmon is a good friend of mine and one of the partners in our organization. He's one of those guys who love the project plans and the data. He's good for our organization, with his analytical and evaluative mind, and our organization is good for him. He has recently started to lead a brand-new division within SVI. As he and I were discussing the start of this division, I remember asking him to just imagine what this division should look like. I told him that I didn't want to see any plans during his first sixty days in the role; I just wanted him to understand the business of that division and to get familiar with the landscape. I also wanted him to dream about what this division could be and what it could mean to SVI.

The assignment was a stretch for him because it involved imagination and invention from scratch. Tim is a left-brained guy, and he was going to have to be intentional about working his right brain. To do so, he changed his setting—hanging diagrams and models on his usually very clean and untouched walls. He started the planning process by shunning the spreadsheet; instead, he created visuals on a blank sheet of paper. This left-brained, analytical processor began to find significant value in doodling. And eventually, his plan started to leap out from the previously blank canvas; Tim started with some really big brush strokes (ideas) and then eventually filled in some details.

Tim is off and running, and the potential for this division is exciting. He'll admit that he still isn't entirely comfortable using his imagination to conjure up new things. It will always be a conscious effort for him. He has to work at it. The way he works at it is by changing his setting—to a quiet and creative space, absent of spreadsheets and project plans. And he's adopting a few tools, such as using a blank sheet of paper for doodling, and reading interesting articles without a highlighter.

What's your ideal place? If you're like me, then your imagination can be easily interrupted by the slightest disruption. My phone distracts me, my email distracts me, and a far-off conversation can completely capture my mind. Therefore I have to find the place where my mind can escape and begin to dream. Rarely is that place at my office—that's way too busy. I usually have to be alone to imagine. My creative place can be my hotel room while I'm traveling for business or my home office above my garage. If I need to be imaginative, and my creative mind is blocked, I escape. I switch my setting. That works for me, but not for everyone. Other people have that one single or special place where their creativity flows. It could be crowded or isolated, silent or bustling—whatever works for them.

Do you know the setting in which you are most imaginative and creative, or have you settled for left-brained thinking only? If you haven't invested the time for imagination, then find a place and time to do just that. Don't underestimate the impact and influence of your setting. Pick your spot or spots and commit to growing your right brain.

To become a more imaginative and creative leader, take on a few of the recommendations from this chapter:

- Tap the power of your mental energy with right-brained, wide-open, creative thinking before whittling down an idea to make it fit in every detail and limitation. Use your analytical left brain to filter your imaginative ideas, not to stifle a healthy start to the creative-thinking process.

- Don't allow your imaginings to become fantasy. Make sure that your imaginative efforts are targeted toward an objective and that your ideas, though difficult, are at least possible.

- Put some effort behind your imagination. Be intentional about your imaginative, creative-thinking time, and plan it into your day or your week. Work at it even when you don't really feel entirely creative.

- Identify a place or places where you can go to actively dream. Make sure your setting is conducive to creative, wide-open thinking—inspiring to you, limiting distractions from others.

13

BECOME INCLUSIVE

When I was considering starting my own company, I had a vision for where I wanted to go and what I wanted it to be. But I knew that vision alone doesn't make a great organization. Before embarking on the long road to founding SVI, I accessed a bunch of resources to help vet and validate my idea. I met with many different people inside and outside of the organizational development industry. I read every book and article I could get my hands on. I wanted to be an expert on organizational development, training, consulting, leadership—everything I'd need to make my firm the best it could be. But I also went outside of the industry. I talked with friends and strangers. I gained ideas from the entertainment and advertising industries. I traveled to a few places I had never been to before in order to get a better glimpse of the world and the people in it. I asked what makes them tick, how they are inspired, and what experiences truly move and change them at their core.

Believe it or not, two movies had a powerful impact on the development of SVI—*Joe Versus the Volcano*, with Tom Hanks and Meg Ryan, and *The Game*, featuring Michael Douglas. *Joe Versus the Volcano* gave me the inspiration to do something that could change people at their core, and *The Game* gave me some ideas for how to drive such change.

Both of these movies highlighted significant life experiences for the main characters. Tom Hanks, as Joe, didn't start living until he realized he was dying. And Michael Douglas's character, Nicholas Van Orton, was a depressed billionaire who wanted to die, until he started running for his life. From these movies, I realized that crucible experiences—testing and tragic experiences—can really drive deep-rooted change. When I lost my son, Blake, to leukemia, I was humbled and crushed like never before. I still maintain an element of brokenness from that experience that will never heal. My memories of Blake make me more humble—and more adventurous. They remind me that I'm not that big of a deal, and that life is short.

As I thought about the movie *The Game*, I realized that a highly successful person would have a hard time changing behavior through a simple training program. They probably wouldn't invest in a development concept with cute activities and rubber chicken for lunch. A life coach might be interesting, but I couldn't think of a way to balance my personal ineptness with a career that tells others how to live their lives. But look at the change that came about for Nicholas Van Orton after he ran for his life. He went from depressed to ecstatic—high on life. Therefore, the first product that SVI ever put out, and is still working with today, is called Radical Sabbatical—yes, this is the same Radical Sabbatical that I referenced in Chapter Eight.

In this program we take executives and put them in the middle of the rain forests of Costa Rica. These executives experience discomfort and challenge such as they've never experienced before—but at a level that they can relate to. It is extreme and intense on a cognitive, emotional, and physically challenging level. Radical Sabbatical was born out of our desire to create an experience that forced executives into an alien environment, but then landed them safely on solid ground. It is an experience that lasts in their memory for their lifetime and significantly affects their leadership. And the idea was born of two movies. Talk about uncommon resources.

To grow your own resourcefulness, you must learn to be inclusive. Not just of uncommon resources, but of opposing ideas, different perspectives, and new ways of thinking and of doing things. These are among the most vital and valuable resources for an Anywhere Leader.

To be inclusive means to include many things or everything. To be inclusive as an Anywhere Leader means that you go beyond yourself to gain access to a lot of things from a lot of places and a lot of people. But how does one put down her pride, her hard-won expertise, and a lifetime of specialized knowledge to connect with others and learn to learn from other valuable sources? Let's talk about ways to develop a more inclusive nature.

Recommendation #1: Invest

Resources don't just come to you as if you're some kind of magnet. Just as you don't wait for inspiration, you don't wait for people, ideas, or materials to come to you. You go after them.

Gathering relational resources is extremely difficult for some. After all, who wants to seek someone out? Don't we want to be sought after? Don't we want to be the ones pursued? We have egos to protect, don't we?

Should I call him?
Shouldn't he call me?
If I call him, then he'll think I need him.
Fine, I'll call him. But I'm not comfortable with this.

Hi, David. I'd love to learn more about your experience leading the project team in South America. Can we get coffee when you've got time?

Oh, great. He thinks I'm an idiot and don't know what I'm doing.

OK. There may be some sort of small risk or hit to your ego in asking for help, advice, time, or perspective. But the first thing Anywhere Leaders learn to do is put aside their own egos. They are more for progress than for personal protection or ego-stroking. They don't wait for others to inquire; they take the initiative to be the reachER, not the reachEE. They make the call.

Consider your own habits. Do you swallow your pride and actively seek out the help of others? When you have an idea that you think might be something great, do you hoard it, afraid to seek honest criticism, or do you ask others to do their best to shine the harsh light of contradiction on it (on you)? How many times have you dared to venture outside of your comfort zone to seek the information you need? Do you instead just let it come to you?

Take on some additional risk: Seek out others for help. Inquire more. Be willing to ask others for help even when you think your credibility might take a hit. Fight the urge to sit inside of your silo until you figure things out for yourself just so you can prove that you didn't need the help. Those who draw in collaboration will move with much greater speed and with much greater effectiveness that those who protect their egos by waiting to be pursued.

Engaging others and identifying abundant resources takes investment on your part. Just as you have to put time into imagination, you need to invest in understanding who and what are accessible as potential resources. You've got to talk with more people, read more things, observe more actions, mine new data, and seek new information.

Your investment into others isn't just about building a relationship with them. It's about investing in them and going further with them, deeper. It means learning about them—their interests, needs, and capabilities—and being more vulnerable with them. Why? Because these relationships form the network on which your career will fail or rise, a network with massive value—as long as it is managed with respect and collaborative wisdom. Yes, I've got lots of contacts—phone numbers and email addresses of people I know. But I could never exploit them as a valuable resource for my own ends alone. The fact that each is a contact gives me only limited access. From many people in my network, I will ask for help on surface needs and easy-to-accomplish items. But when I'm in a tight spot and I need some real support, I'd better have a few of those relationships that I have invested in deeply. I'd better have a few people I can call on for just about anything. That kind of relationship requires personal investment.

How about your relationships—do you have a few or many relationships that you can count on for your deepest support needs? Do you have those "go to" people in whom you've invested and who have invested in you, or have most of your relationships come about through glad-handing and business card sharing at a few social functions?

If you've got more of the latter type, then I encourage you to start identifying people in whom you can invest more deeply—people you can champion and who can champion you. Spend more time with people who think differently, with different experiences and different backgrounds, and who can broaden your insights and ideas. Be more open with them. Understand people and their needs. Bring value to them and their agendas. Do this, and they will likely be there for you in return, with a better understanding of your needs and what they can do to help you.

Anywhere Leaders know how to use their diverse and broad relationships. But they're also amazing at gathering all kinds of resources (not just people), because they journey through more avenues of information. Whereas others limit their access to industry-specific information only, resourceful Anywhere Leaders are inclusive of other industry resources as well. These leaders aren't stuck in the red oceans of industry-oriented and business-as-usual information; they venture out to blue oceans of opportunity for their knowledge-gathering. The blue oceans are the uncharted waters where new opportunities exist. Leaders who discover them aren't satisfied with knowing what everyone else in their profession knows; they venture out into other industries, hoping to discover new connections and insights. My industry is organizational development (OD), but in addition to OD publications, I read up on entertainment, technology, digital media, and advertising to give me breakthrough ideas that haven't been considered in OD. I mentioned Bill Gates in Chapter Eight—he's a businessman who reads about medicine, chemistry, and linguistics. And he finds business value in every one of these areas. His investment in these topics broadens his access. How about you? What are you investing in to broaden your access—more outside-of-industry subscriptions, new books, and the occasional weekend seminar to develop a new craft? Are you participating in more conversations, making comments to bloggers you follow inside and outside of your industry? Are you testing more tools and systems? Are you being more inclusive of resources or working to limit your knowledge inputs?

Read more things, test more things, learn more things. Some of you may be saying, "No way, Mike. My plate is already overloaded." I understand. But increasing access isn't about adding burden. It's about structuring your life so that you're fully accessible to what's around you. I'll talk more about how you can do this without getting overwhelmed in Chapter Seventeen.

Recommendation #2: Leverage Access

Resourceful leaders have greater access to information because they've invested in capturing it. When these leaders invest in

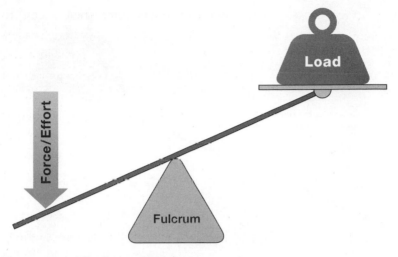

Figure 13.1 The Lever Model

capturing diverse and broad resources, then they are in a better position to use those resources to fulfill business objectives. Imagine a simple lever and fulcrum—the kind studied in your high school physics class. On one side of the scale you've got the load. The load is your obstacle: the seemingly impossible goal or task that, without a little leverage, you have no hope of moving. It sits on or is carried by the lever. Beneath the midpoint of the lever is the fulcrum, which acts as the pivot point for the action. Counter to the load is the opposing mechanical force or effort. This force is usually you and your resources. As shown in Figure 13.1, enough force or effort can get the job done.

Now let's relabel these components to make the model more relevant to the business setting and to show how it applies to an Anywhere Leader's ability to lift a greater load or take on larger work challenges (see Figure 13.2).

Viewing this model, we can see that in order to lift (overcome) a work challenge, a business leader must lever with the weight of her resources, using team knowledge, skills, and experiences as the fulcrum. If the challenge is great, then the most direct way to overcome it is to channel *more resources* into the problem. When

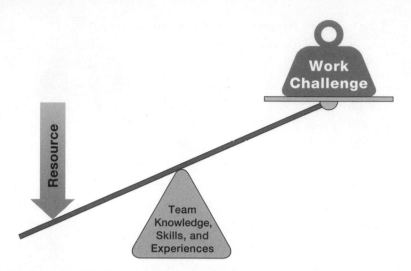

Figure 13.2 The Leadership Lever Model

we gather and apply more resources, we can "lift" (carry) more workload or tackle greater work problems. But how can you make this model work for you to help you apply more resources to your work challenges? And if putting more resources into the problem is the most direct solution, what are some indirect solutions for those of us—all of us—who don't have unlimited resources?

In the model there are three elements that you can adjust or alter to achieve a good result. To make things easier, consider the formulas that relate to this model:

1. High access to resources × ideal configuration of team knowledge, skills, and experiences = ability to overcome considerable work challenges

2. High access to resources × poor configuration of team knowledge, skills, and experiences = ability to overcome average work challenges

3. Low access to resources × ideal configuration of team knowledge, skills, and experiences = ability to overcome average work challenges

4. Low access to resources × poor configuration of team knowledge, skills, and experiences = ability to overcome only minimal work challenges

The Anywhere Leader works these formulas for effective outcomes. For example, if she is leading an unproven, untested, and inexperienced team, she has two options: lighten the workload (which she likely won't do) or increase her access to resources. If she wants to meet the enormous business challenge with an inexperienced team, she is going to have to access relationships (resources) that she can use—those people who can truly lend a hand. When the challenge is big and the capabilities are low, this leader better be great at accessing an abundance of resources: new information, new people, new tools, new capacity, and new capabilities (see Figure 13.3).

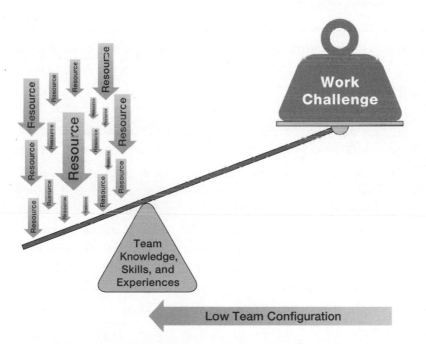

Figure 13.3 The Leadership Lever Model: Poor Team Configuration, Abundant Resources

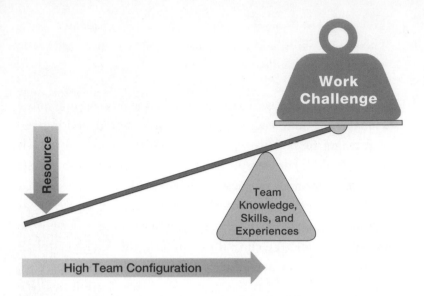

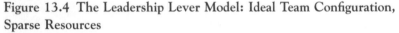

Figure 13.4 The Leadership Lever Model: Ideal Team Configuration, Sparse Resources

If the access to resources is low, then the Anywhere Leader knows to align with a good, knowledgeable, and experienced team to take on the heavy challenge. In this scenario, the fulcrum must move to the right—toward the challenge end (see Figure 13.4).

If there's no access to abundant resources and the team is inexperienced and lacks knowledge and skill, then a good leader figures out a way to either reduce the workload or take on a smaller challenge.

Anywhere Leaders aren't entirely dependent on highly skilled and knowledgeable teams. They are often put in places where teams are struggling. And more often than not, an Anywhere Leader's workload is a hefty one with significant business challenges. Anywhere Leaders are used to leading with the following calculation: *High access to resources × poor configuration of team knowledge, skills, and experiences = ability to overcome average work challenges.*

It's important to point out, however, that Anywhere Leaders don't just bank on the help from inclusive relationships they've

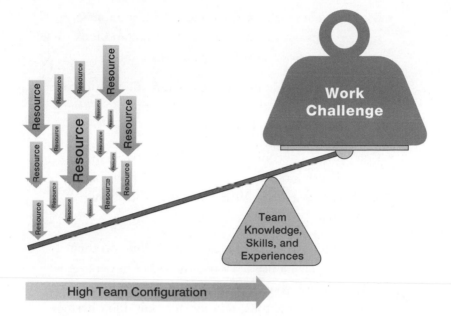

Figure 13.5 The Leadership Lever Model: Ideal Team Configuration, Abundant Resources

made in the past or on any number of material resources that are available to them. They also go to work to develop the limited knowledge, skills, and experience of their teams. They want to use all of their resources and rapidly develop their own teams— *maximum access × ideal configuration of team knowledge, skills, and experiences*—so that they can successfully take on the toughest challenges and meet the most demanding goals (see Figure 13.5).

Create your own leverage model. Is your workload heavy? If so, are you fortunate to have a team with the necessary knowledge, skills, and experience, or are you relying on your inclusion of and access to resources? Do you have access to the resources needed to overcome the challenges of your current workload? What changes do you need to make in order to be more effective in achieving success by mastering tough work challenges?

As you work to become more inclusive, consider implementing the following recommendations:

- Broaden your reach for resources. Develop more relationships outside of your organization, and look to gain insights from outside of your own industry.

- Be more vulnerable in your leadership. Be willing to be the one to ask others for help rather than waiting to be the one pursued for help.

- Don't just make contacts with others—invest in them. Know more about their interests, their needs, and their capabilities. When you invest in them, they'll likely invest in you, too.

- Be willing to use your relationships, calling on them when you have a need. Don't shy away from engaging others because you don't want to feel like you're being a burden. Don't abuse a relationship, but don't hesitate to use it during times of need, either.

- Be careful not to be inclusive of your external resources yet not inclusive of your own team. An Anywhere Leader works her resources and develops the capabilities of her internal team to tackle the toughest challenges.

14

BECOME INVENTIVE

If imagination draws on the right side of the brain, inventive thinking harnesses our left brain to take our imagination and put engineering behind it—what Disney calls "imagineering."

There is so much talk of the need for adaptive leaders today. Why? Because these adaptive leaders can shift and adjust to the changing demands of today's business landscape. But the Anywhere Leader goes further than just being adaptive. He is inventive, and his ability to invent—to create solutions that just didn't previously exist—makes him more than adaptable. It makes him resourceful. Sure, Anywhere Leaders are adaptable, but they can also make *things* adaptable through their ability to invent. Because they leverage their resources to create solutions, adaptability becomes more than a leadership skill; it becomes an engineering advantage as well. These leaders can change, and they can change things. The question is, how?

Recommendation #1: Become a Tinkerer

I can't help but envision the mad scientists at work here—banging with tools, lighting a few things that blow up in their face, burning off their eyebrows. I imagine these types of inventors in a laboratory hammering away at a bunch of metal, rarely creating anything that works. For managers, the comparison goes only so far. If we started blowing up our laboratories in a business environment, we'd be kicked out the door. We know business managers must take care not to damage existing business, clients, or colleagues in the interest of innovation. We can't be mad geniuses unless that's in our contract. If my business saw me exhibiting such irrational behavior, I'd surely be labeled, and a succession plan would move up on the priority list. We need to tinker *effectively*.

So how do you tinker in the business environment without destroying your reputation as a steady and solid performer? In my observation, great leaders and executives always seem to have a pet project or two going on. They've always got their base business with base responsibilities, but they are also testing a few new ideas on the side. Many call these "skunkworks"—after the trademarked Skunk Works of Lockheed Martin Advanced Development Programs. "Skunkworks" is used generically to refer to advanced or even somewhat secret projects that may not align with current business strategy or an existing revenue stream. For Lockheed Martin, Skunk Works was responsible for some of their most significant aircraft inventions, such as the U-2 spy plane, the SR-71 that found its way into spaceflight, and the F-22 Raptor. Some of the greatest inventions have begun as "skunkworks" projects by business leaders or executives. The Anywhere Leader needs to nurture her "skunkworks" but remember her *real works*.

Although they rarely blow things up, these leaders establish some testing and trial opportunities. They may even ask the organization for a few resources to help them further develop these pet projects, hoping to establish a way-out advantage for the business. Cornerstone OnDemand is one of the leading learning management system (LMS) designers in our industry. Their CEO, Adam Miller, is responsible for running Cornerstone OnDemand in a sound, responsible manner. Even so, Miller started a pet project on the side called CyberU—a low-cost, highly flexible alternative to high-cost and highly complex LMSs—a project that, in some ways, even competes with his own company. CyberU is bringing significant innovation to the training and development industry— and creating some pretty amazing advantages for Cornerstone OnDemand.

Regardless of whether your pet project works inside or outside your corporate structure and strategy, the key is to adopt some sort of "skunkworks" project. Tinker a little.

Take a moment to ask yourself: *Do I have a pet project that stirs my passion—maybe even one that doesn't align with the organization's immediate interests? What am I doing in my off hours that provides insight into my invention? Am I working on the next big thing (or even the next little thing)? If so, what is the next step?*

If you have no such pet project in the works, identify something that fascinates you or perplexes you about your business. Try to define it—noodle with it a little. When you think you've got a decent understanding and some passion behind an idea, pitch it to your organization or your team as a potential "skunkworks" project. Remember, however, that "skunkworks" projects should not steer you away from your real works projects. You may have to find pet projects on your own time. If you pitch such a project well, you may convince your organization to throw some resources your way. Whether or not your company accepts it, tinkering is important. You will likely be amazed at what you learn in the process—and maybe even be a little surprised by what can be accomplished.

Recommendation #2: Stand on the Shoulders of Giants

Inventors embrace the idea that they stand on the shoulders of giants. Meaning that they never started from scratch as they created their inventions—they picked up from where some other inventor left off. They don't reinvent the wheel, but embrace the fact that the wheel was invented before the bicycle, electricity was invented before the light bulb, and adhesives were invented before the Band-Aid.

Anywhere Leaders take what's already there and build on it. Because of their discernment, they have the ability to take what is good and discard the other stuff—for a newer, greater invention. An extraordinary amount of accomplishment in this world is based on keeping the grain and discarding the chaff.

Inventive leaders love the idea of versions 2.0, 3.0, 4.0, and beyond into a future fostered by practical innovation and predictable magic. The World Wide Web started as a way to passively view enormous amounts of content online. Web 2.0 inventors added greater interactivity, collaboration, social media, user-generated content, and virtual community. These 2.0 inventors built on the first generation of the Web.

Sometimes when we think about our inventions, we want the full credit, the full glory—the "no one in the world has ever thought of this" idea or the "world will never be the same again" idea. But few inventions are world-changers.

To see whether you're benefiting from the wisdom of previous generations, ask yourself, honestly: *Am I standing on the shoulders of giants, or am I in pursuit of that one invention that would bring me full and exclusive glory? Am I making things difficult by mandating that every part and process be my own creation, or am I using the thoughts and efforts of those who came before me? When the time comes to receive praise for my success, will I be resentful if I have to share credit with others, or am I strong enough to pass the praise around?*

If you're an Anywhere Leader, you are more effective because you are keen to what's already there and focused on how to build on that foundation of greatness.

Recommendation #3: Don't Work Off of Old Assumptions

The Artist Formerly Known as Prince was a person who reinvented himself and became merely a symbol. Odd, but OK. Society says you need an identity; Prince decided to go without one and become not-Prince. Society had its assumptions, but the Artist Formerly Known as Prince had his own—and they worked for him. He captured headlines and pumped out records and forced society to deal with him on his terms. Not that this illustration has much to do with invention, but it does highlight how some people are able to drive growth and progress by not working or living according to the assumptions of others.

Inventors, by definition, live outside the assumptions of others, and they are often seen as a little eccentric. Why? Because they dare to question the things that everyone else takes for granted. Inventive leaders don't always succumb to perceived standards or status—in fact, they take them as a challenge. They love to crush dogmatic thinking.

It's unlikely that we can be the *Princes* of our business—extravagant and controversial. Some standards are good—when they enable desired results. Anywhere Leaders break from standards only when they become barriers to growth and progress. Maybe that's what separates these inventors. They don't waste time wishing for different standards or more resources. They don't excuse themselves from subpar results because things weren't set up right for them. They get to inventing—quickly. When an inventive leader's budget gets cut by seven figures, he doesn't give up and say, "My hands are tied." He creates new assumptions and gets to work.

When a noninventive leader says, "I can never deliver my 25-percent revenue growth goal when my advertising budget has been cut in half," that noninventive leader is making an assumption that there is a direct relationship between the ad budget and revenue growth. The inventive leader is charged by the challenge; she starts to form new assumptions by tinkering with some "what if" and "why not" scenarios. In this example, the inventive leader finds ways to find residual income through existing product lines. The inventive leader doesn't just assume that the primary demographic is twenty-five- to fifty-four-year-old males. She expands the product's relevance to moms as well.

Simply put, these inventive leaders don't always try to change the limits; rather, they try to change the problem—and they do so by forcing a personal shift in assumptions thinking. Because of it, they confidently attempt the things that seem impossible.

Are you focused on limitations and restrictions—making them an excuse for results? Are you adopting standards and assumptions that are barriers to progress? When did you last act by defying the assumptions of others? When your budget is reduced, do you give up on your goals? When your team is downsized, do you punt on your strategies? Or do you rethink to reinvent? What assumptions are getting in the way of better results? Where can you begin to shift your assumptions and take on a more inventive mindset?

To become a more inventive leader, engage in some of the recommendations from this chapter:

- Tinker with your pet projects and encourage your subordinates to do the same. Encourage a culture of wild experimentation, and advance those side interests that may not immediately appear related to your organization's core competencies. If the idea shows merit, you may create new market opportunities.

- Don't be afraid to stand on the shoulders of giants. Every great innovation is built on the inventions of others, and it is arrogant to think that you can do it alone. Likewise, remember to give credit where it is due.

- Amazing things happen when you start to question your own assumptions. So many great opportunities have been missed because people assumed that their ideas weren't possible, probable, or cost-efficient.

Add the elements from an imaginative and inclusive leader, and you will easily develop into a resourceful leader. Add the resourceful leader to the curious leader who is driven for progress, and you will easily develop into an Anywhere Leader.

The rest of this book will be dedicated to providing you with recommendations and helpful tools that you can apply to accommodate you in your journey to becoming an Anywhere Leader.

Part Five

APPLICATION FOR THE ANYWHERE LEADER

15

THE MECHANICS OF THE ANYWHERE LEADER MODEL

For this book to be truly valuable, the concepts, ideas, and recommendations that have been featured up until now must have a place to land—a workable base. For the Anywhere Leader, this workable base comes in the form of a model. But whereas many models are conceptual in nature, I wanted to go one step further and create one that is *mechanical* as well. (Blame the tinkerer in me.) In other words, the Anywhere Leader model must be capable of being moved, flexed, and adjusted—just as people who are developing themselves as more alert leaders can move, flex, and adjust. The model must accommodate various inputs and outputs that provide insights precisely tailored to the one and only you. The insights you gain from the Anywhere Leader model are designed for one simple, ambitious purpose: to help you lead and perform better when faced with uncertainty.

Let's start right now: Do you find yourself in conditions of uncertainty? Are you in a leadership role that forces you to navigate the unknown? Are you constantly dealing with change coming at you from all different directions—or are you in the driver's seat of major change initiatives? If so, then the Anywhere Leader model should be a valuable tool for you to use to grow your leadership capabilities to be more effective in uncertain and unfamiliar conditions. But for those of you in roles that are pretty predictable and fairly consistent, this model can illustrate how nicely you align with your role—helping you grow in confidence.

After all, not everyone is an Anywhere Leader or needs to be. Many managers and business leaders, on taking an assessment of their Anywhere Leader traits and strengths, would score lower than they'd expected. But that is OK, because not everyone operates in a workplace that requires an Anywhere Leader's distinctive skills. If Bob is *not* an Anywhere Leader—let's say he scores as a Level One (out of ten)—then the last place he should be working is a job fit for a Level Nine Anywhere Leader. In that same vein, he is *perfectly* suited to work in jobs that are relatively stable and secure—the kind of positions that would make an Anywhere Leader go nuts. In the next chapter, I'll spend a little more time discussing how to judge the stability of a job and how to measure the level of uncertainty in your environment.

Recall the three traits of the Anywhere Leader Model: driven for progress, sensationally curious, and vastly resourceful. When I began looking at what makes an alert, adaptive, and truly *anywhere* leader, I didn't just pick the traits out of the ether. They have been identified from numerous research studies as valuable leadership characteristics that help individuals, teams, and organizations perform during times of uncertainty. (Remember "standing on the shoulders of giants"?) Though I use slightly different terms, these traits are supported in the works of psychologists and management scholars such as Young and Dulewicz (2006); Judge, Naoumova, and Douglas (2009); and Kirkpatrick and Locke (1991)—just to name a few.[1] These traits have been shown time and again to have a strong positive correlation with a leader's performance in uncertain scenarios. Leaders who exhibit these traits are more likely to outperform others when operating in uncertain situations.

Because there is already so much work supporting the impact of these traits on performance in uncertainty, one might say: *Mike, this is the same old story.* But the Anywhere Leader model wasn't created simply to remind leaders of the importance of being driven for progress, sensationally curious, or vastly resourceful—I wanted to *build* on that foundation. Sure, our research validates existing findings, but that was never the point.

What *was* the point?

First, I wanted the Anywhere Leader model to package the findings of previous great minds and communicate them in an easy-to-understand way. So much knowledge and opportunity is lost because we don't have the time to thumb through a half dozen research journals every night before bed. Second, and more important, I recognized that although so many of us are expected to be masters of uncertainty—perfectly comfortable and capable of handling life's sudden twists—no one had developed a way to help those of us who aren't so flexible to become a *little* more comfortable and a *little* more capable.

Does your job throw you curveballs that make you stressed? Here's a book on how to cope with stress! You need to set up shop in a new country, a new culture, and you have only six months to turn a profit? Sure, you've got experts, advisers, and mentors aplenty. But what if you want to be more comfortable with uncertainty, or grow in your capacity to tackle change? Not so much.

The Anywhere Leader model supports an individual's personal development toward becoming a better performer in today's modern world—in which things aren't certain or predictable. The Anywhere Leader model helps people develop into their desired job. It is designed to help individuals assess how ideally they are suited for their target job and, if they aren't suited, easily determine what it would take to get there. Ultimately, it is a developmental model that can be used to support and measure your growing capabilities to lead anywhere.

With the Anywhere Leader model, individuals can compare their current ability to lead in uncertain or unfamiliar conditions with the level of ability needed for their target or ideal job. For example, if your leadership capabilities are best suited for a fairly defined and predictable role, then your target job might be a job similar to that of a bank teller or assembly line operator. However, if you want to grow your capabilities to be suited for a corporate vice-president position—a job that demands that you effectively lead in many different cultures with many different standards and norms and through economic fluctuations—then the Anywhere Leader model can help you make progress toward such a role.

So if the three traits—driven for progress, sensationally curious, and vastly resourceful—are important to performing in the midst of uncertainty, then it's important to understand how the specific strengths of each trait serve to enhance the impact of these traits. These strengths don't represent the components of drive, curiosity, or resourcefulness. Rather, they are separate personal characteristics that interact with an Anywhere Leader's drive, curiosity, and resourcefulness to produce the performance gains needed in complex and uncertain situations.

Remember, an Anywhere Leader's drive is different from the typical leader's drive. The Anywhere Leader's drive is based on integrity—doing the good and the right thing even when doing the good and the right thing is harder. For the Anywhere Leader, the effects of this drive are made stronger by the fact that she makes the smart call (discerning), takes the bold move (daring), and holds on to her plan (determined), not for ease and individual benefit alone, but for progress.

An Anywhere Leader's curiosity is different from typical curiosity. Anywhere Leaders' curiosity is born of looking within and then inviting others to share in their own insights. For the Anywhere

Leader, curiosity is pursued by being reflective, receptive, and perceptive.

It's the same with resourcefulness—it's moving from adaption to invention. By bringing imagination, inclusiveness, and inventiveness to the table, the Anywhere Leader is able to accomplish the job when the job appears impossible. Figure 15.1 shows the alignment between the Anywhere Leader's traits and strengths.

These strengths magnify the positive relationship between a leader's personal traits and his performance when faced with an uncertain or novel situation. By developing Anywhere Leader strengths, an individual becomes capable of leading the business and others confidently across the changing terrain of today's economic landscape.

Basic Mechanics

First, let's focus on the mechanics of the traits. As you may have noticed, the traits of an Anywhere Leader are split into three equal bands on the model globe, from the northernmost band (driven for progress) to the southernmost band (vastly resourceful). A person with a perfect balance of these three traits can be depicted with a globe whose bands are similarly in perfect balance, as in Figure 15.2.

Alas, few things in life are perfect, so perfect balance is highly unlikely. Most people are more naturally gifted in one trait or have developed one trait over another. In examining the model, the vertical span of the band representing each trait communicates how much you embody a particular trait. To better illustrate the point, let's look at a few examples of how these traits may be unbalanced—showing a particular trait being stronger than another. Remember Thomas in Chapter One, who was not an Anywhere Leader? His profile appears in Figure 15.3.

The varied heights among the trait bands on this model represent areas where a leader either has already developed a trait (the

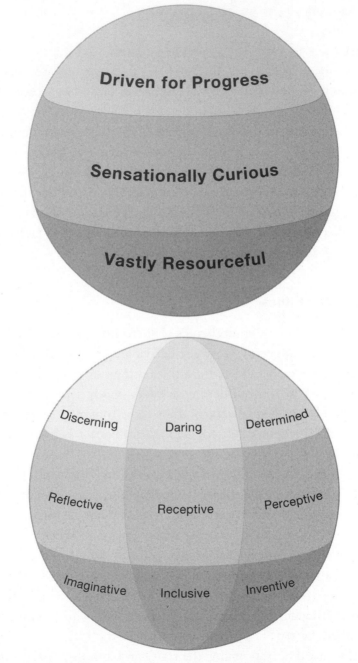

Figure 15.1 Three Core Traits and Behavioral Strengths of the Anywhere Leader

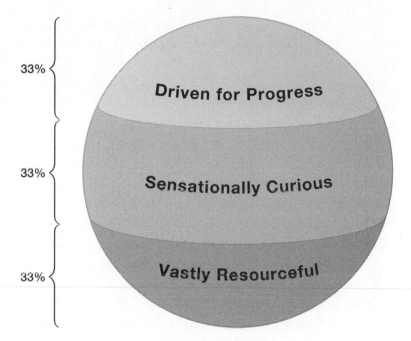

Figure 15.2 Three Core Traits: Perfectly Balanced

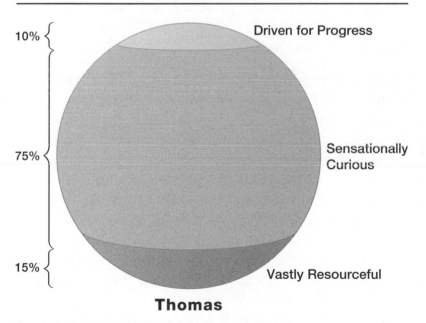

Figure 15.3 Three Core Traits: Thomas's Profile

broader bands) or needs to focus some attention (the more narrow bands). Clearly, Thomas excels at curiosity, but his zest for the unknown comes at the cost of his drive for progress and overall resourcefulness. He should consider putting some focus on developing his drive and resourcefulness if he wants to become Anywhere Leader material.

That's Thomas. What about you? How do you score yourself?

Take a moment and ask yourself: *How do these three traits rank in my leadership? Am I more driven for progress than I am sensationally curious? Am I more resourceful than I am driven for progress? When I read through the previous chapters, which trait did I identify with the most? Do I have a pretty good balance of all three traits?*

Your answers don't have to be scientifically sound. You probably know enough about yourself and your tendencies to ballpark it. If you're struggling to label yourself here, then by all means visit the Anywhere Leader website (www.anywhereleader.com) and take the assessment to help you validate and confirm your tendencies.

Moderation Mechanics

The three-part model presented in these figures represents the foundation of Anywhere Leadership. The vertical span of each trait band is determined by the proportion of that trait in comparison to the other two. Next, the strengths associated with each trait are added to the model. As shown in Figure 15.4, each strength is shown within its associated trait, and the comparative size of that strength is represented by the width of its segment. The Anywhere Leader model demonstrates how the traits fit together with their related strengths by aligning them in horizontal bands, the strengths separated vertically with light-to-dark shading. In interpreting the complete Anywhere Leader model, it is important to remember that *balance* is your goal. Just as you sought a balance of traits (represented by those visually appealing equal-sized horizontal

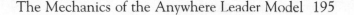

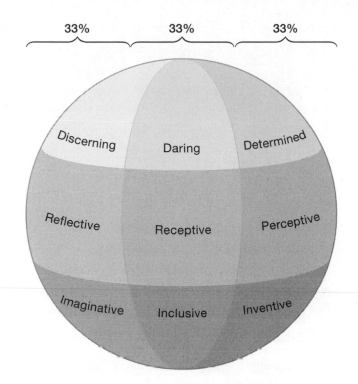

Figure 15.4 Behavioral Strengths: Perfectly Balanced

bands), you want a balance of strengths (represented by equally appealing same-size vertical sections).

As the proportional span of the band depicts the level of a particular trait exhibited by a leader, so does the width of a section represent the leader's proficiency in that strength. It's typical for a leader to either be more naturally gifted in a particular strength or to have invested more time developing a particular strength. Individuals like to differentiate themselves from the crowd, and one way to do that is to gain mastery in one specific trait or ability. This is human nature, and for 99 percent of the population it makes perfect sense. But for the Anywhere Leader, balance of strengths is important. Recall that a daring leader without discernment is reckless, and that being receptive to others without being personally reflective removes your own personal and valuable

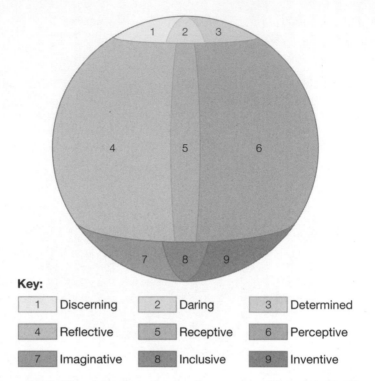

Key:

1	Discerning	2	Daring	3	Determined
4	Reflective	5	Receptive	6	Perceptive
7	Imaginative	8	Inclusive	9	Inventive

Figure 15.5 The Anywhere Leader Assessment: Thomas's Profile

experience that could be relevant to an issue you're trying to address. Your imaginative nature without the ability to invent makes you a dreamer with no ability to execute and implement your ideas.

Let's have a look at Thomas again, showing the relative proportions of his strengths (see Figure 15.5). Unfortunately, his Anywhere Leader model is almost completely out of balance in *both* traits and strengths.

While Thomas's diagram presents a rather alarming imbalance, it helps him identify areas that need attention. Aspiring Anywhere Leaders identify the smaller strength sections and work to develop in those areas first, secure in the knowledge that they have room to grow into a better balance with those areas that dominate their profile.

How do you score yourself on these strengths?
Take another moment and ask yourself:

- How do these nine strengths rank in my leadership?

- Do I lack discernment to support my daring nature?

- Do I contemplate solutions within my own mind without inquiring for the opinions of others emphasizing my personal reflection over my receptivity?

- Do I have a pretty good balance of all of these strengths?

Again, your answers don't have to be scientifically sound. Ballpark it. However, if this is a struggle for you, the Anywhere Leader assessment at www.anywhereleader.com can take you through a series of questions that have been validated in order to accurately capture your Anywhere Leader strengths as well.

Development Mechanics

At this point you may well be thinking, *Mike, this is all well and good, but how do I know if I've got enough of the Anywhere Leader traits and behavioral strengths to be effective in uncertain environments? Is balance all there is to being a great leader?* Excellent point. In order to know if you are enough of an Anywhere Leader to handle a job of great uncertainty, you need to identify two things: (1) how much of an Anywhere Leader you currently are (based on the preceding pages) and (2) how much of a role uncertainty plays in your job.

The greater the balance you achieve among the traits, the stronger your foundation of leadership capability is for dealing with environmental uncertainty. But that is not enough. You must build on those traits by honing your strengths once you've targeted a job that requires you to lead through the unfamiliar. But the job is important as well and should not be forgotten. Let's say you want to take a Level One job—a job that has very little environmental uncertainty. In that case, scoring consistently low on all nine strengths indicates that you're perfectly suited for that Level One job. But what about a Level Nine job, where unpredictability and change are far more common than what you're used to? As shown in Figure 15.6, in that case, your Anywhere Leader model will reflect the gap between your current strength configuration (at Level One) and your target job's requirements (at Level Nine).

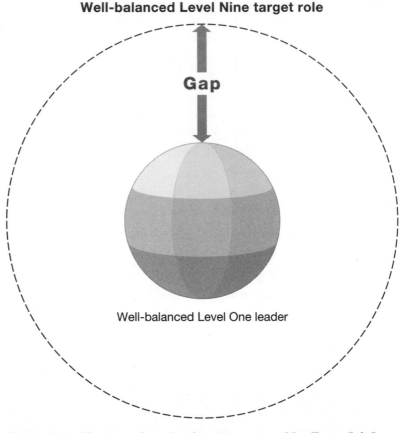

Figure 15.6 The Anywhere Leader Assessment: Not Every Job Is an Anywhere Leader Job

The point of this book is to equip you to become an Anywhere Leader, fully capable of performing successfully in high uncertainty and unfamiliar jobs—jobs for Anywhere Leaders. Therefore, it is important to identify your target or desired job, identify the level of uncertainty associated with the job, and then determine your ability to align with the job. The Anywhere Leader model helps you identify certain deficiencies and then develop those traits and strengths in order to be most prepared and equipped to succeed in your target job.

Determining Uncertainty

So far, I've focused on basic, moderate, and developmental mechanics of the Anywhere Leader model. I've presented the idea of aligning your abilities with the level of uncertainty required in your target or ideal job. Up to this point, we've focused on the traits and strengths that should be developed for leading in more uncertainty. But how can you determine the level of uncertainty in your desired job? Don't you need to understand both—where you score and what your desired job demands? Absolutely!

A test pilot is in a job of uncertainty. When a test pilot flies a plane for the first time, the pilot has formed many hypotheses of how the plane should react. The pilot has probably spent hours and hours in a simulator trying to prepare for any potential surprises. But until the plane is airborne, hypotheses and predictions remain just that—hypotheses and predictions. In today's environment, we know that we can't completely bank on hypotheses and predictions. There are always going to be a few surprises. Just because the simulation showed a certain fuel burn doesn't mean the actual test flight is going to show the same fuel burn at thirty thousand feet in turbulent air. The test pilot may need to adjust the range based on new information. Just because the aircraft engineers said the plane can handle a significant amount of stress on the aircraft frame during an inverted spin doesn't mean that the plane might not show a few cracks in the process—the test pilot might have to pull out of the inverted spin quicker than had been planned. A test pilot is always evaluating the conditions to see what has changed, to stay ahead of the surprises when possible, and effectively work the surprises when they suddenly appear. In fact, on a scale of 1 to 10, a test pilot's job might just score at the top of the scale in uncertainty.

Contrast the test pilot's role with the role of a bank teller or assembly line worker. These roles are fairly predictable. There isn't much need for an individual to develop daring or discerning skills when the process has been microdefined. For a bank teller, an inventive nature might just get you fired. To use the Anywhere Leader model effectively, you must be able to measure the level of uncertainty required for your job—determining what your targeted job requires of you and your ability to lead through the uncertain and unfamiliar. Let's dive into the next chapter to understand how to evaluate job-level uncertainty requirements.

Note

1. See M. Young and V. Dulewicz, "Leadership Styles, Change Context and Leader Performance in the Royal Navy," *Journal of Change Management*, Vol. 6, No. 4, 383–396 (Routledge, 2006); W. Q. Judge, I. Naoumova, and T. Douglas, "Organizational Capacity for Change and Firm Performance in a Transition Economy," *The International Journal of Human Resource Management*, Vol. 20, No. 8, 1737–1752 (Routledge, Aug. 2009); and S. A. Kirkpatrick and E. A. Locke, "Leadership: Do Traits Matter?" *Academy of Management Executive*, Vol. 5, No. 2, 48–60 (The Academy of Management, 1991).

16

A JOB FOR AN ANYWHERE LEADER?

Have you ever wandered through a fun house at a carnival? When you walk into a fun house, you know you're headed for a lot of mystery and surprises. Things pop out without warning. Floors move and shake. A maze of mirrors gets you completely lost. Mix in a little smoke or fog with a strobe light and you might see people start running in all directions. These are the most popular attractions at amusement parks—the ones that catch us by surprise. And we love them.

Anywhere Leader jobs are a little bit the same, in theory—including the smoke and mirrors. These are jobs where uncertainty is the norm and where there are lots of unknowns, such as having to operate in a new market, with a new crew, with less than the best resources. These jobs aren't easy; rather, they're uneasy and even uncomfortable for a period—maybe even for a long period. Military personnel often find themselves in Anywhere Leader jobs, as they take on new assignments every two or three years in any part of the world. Consultants often find themselves in Anywhere Leader jobs, as they are assigned to a new client every six to ten months before moving on to another client who's quite different from the previous one. But these Anywhere Leader jobs are no longer limited to the soldiers or the consultants. Business leaders in the most storied and stable organizations are finding themselves being moved into uncharted waters for the sake of globalization and competitive advantage. Disruption is the nature of the game today, and the most successful leaders are being thrown into the land of uncertainty and are expected to expertly navigate the unknowns.

Discomfort is inevitable in these unknown conditions. If I'm in a familiar environment, I'm pretty comfortable. Isn't it our human nature to seek safe and comfortable states in life? Even when our stomachs are full, we want to know we have enough food for whenever we get hungry again. Even though we know people all around the world go without the miracle of air conditioning, we in the industrialized nations want to know that we can change that muggy summer day into a cool afternoon with the flip of a switch. And even if we have never come home to find someone else has liberated our hard-earned possessions, we want to know our doors are locked when we are away.

But what an intriguing and complex species we are! Because just as we seek comfort, many of us seek the thrill of uncertainty as well. Too much comfort leads those individuals to restlessness. It's in their fun house nature to test themselves and push their limits. We who share this disposition want to see what we can accomplish and what we are capable of withstanding. So we push ourselves into the unknown by jumping out of airplanes, taking a trip to a foreign country, or joining a new social group. Our senses are more alive in the thrill moments than in the comfort moments, and we like that. Some of us even live for it. Anywhere Leader jobs are thrill jobs, and Anywhere Leaders are geared for them and find them invigorating.

So what are thrill job assignments? They are job assignments where there are lots of unknowns and the potential for a few surprises is fairly high. A thrill job assignment can be highly unpredictable, containing lots of uncertainties. Many scholars have studied environmental uncertainty and the impact that uncertainty—even volatility—has had on a leader's ability to do his job.

In 1984, two of these scholars, Dr. George Dess and Dr. Donald Beard, attempted to measure the concept of uncertainty at an environmental level.[1] Through their research, they identified three components that create environmental uncertainty. Though the terms for these components are very academic (big words), I'll break each of them down and even take some liberty in describing them in my own words.

Environmental Munificence

According to Dess and Beard, one way to measure environmental uncertainty is to look at the richness and abundance of its resources. Imagine being one of the first explorers to find North America. After months at sea, supplies are dwindling, the crew is restless, and even the most experienced sailors have no idea what lies beyond the horizon. In other words, uncertainty is at an all-time high. But, land ho! And, oh, sweet relief: look at all the trees for building with, all the animals for hunting! Although there were still many unknowns, the presence of the right *resources* made their world much more certain.

In other words, when environmental munificence (aka: resource abundance) is low, environmental uncertainty is high. Without the right money, tools, or people on your team, the job of being the best leader for your group becomes significantly more difficult— in part, because the lack of resources severely limits your options in the face of sudden, unforeseen problems. In my own experience, when I don't have enough people to cover a job, then I have questions about how I'm going to get the job done well. When the budget isn't sufficient to thoroughly support an initiative, lots of people begin to question the initiative's potential for success. But resources aren't just dollars and cents; knowledge can be just as important a resource. Observe an inexperienced team, lacking in the right know-how, getting prepped for the start of a complex project, and you may see a lot of head scratching.

Anywhere Leader jobs are jobs with limited resources—low environmental munificence. If you're in an Anywhere Leader job, you likely work within a fairly tight budget, with a team that has limited knowledge or experience, with systems or strategies that are either untested or unproven.

An Anywhere Leader can determine the level of environmental munificence by evaluating three factors: *awareness*, *access*, and *application*.

Let's start with *awareness*. As an Anywhere Leader going into an uncertain environment with entirely new job conditions, you may likely have a limited awareness of what resources are available to you. This is quite different from your job when times were good, in certain and familiar conditions (maybe at corporate HQ), when you knew exactly what resources were available to you: a proven HR department for seeking and selecting qualified employees; a strong base of trusted vendors with whom you'd built strong relationships over the years, who'd helped you grow your knowledge; peers you could count on to hold you accountable; and maybe even a culture that you understood with people who spoke the language you understood as well. Now, in the new, more uncertain environment, you have little awareness of whom you can turn to for advice, what departments you can count on for help, which practices or strategies are most reliable, and what systems will best serve your needs. Anywhere Leaders in an uncertain and unfamiliar environment have less knowledge of what resources are available and valuable to them in their role than they formerly enjoyed (see Figure 16.1).

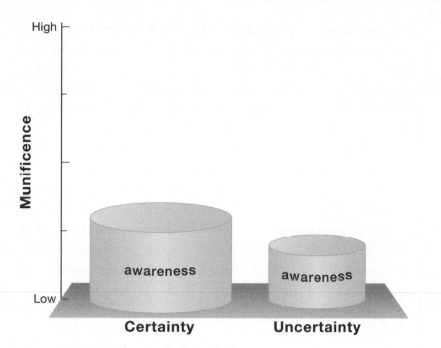

Figure 16.1 Munificence Explained: Awareness

Awareness serves as the base measure for munificence, because the greater our awareness of resources, the more resources we can *access*—which is the second measure of munificence. If I know more, then I also know more of what I can access. My friend Murray, who leads our media group at SVI, has the world's biggest mental bank of music—he is musically aware. Mention a song and he knows it. He can recall thousands of songs, and even though I love music, I'm lucky if I can name twenty-five. Because I have less awareness than he does, it comes as no surprise that I have less access to my internal catalogue of music. I don't know what albums I should buy because I'm not really sure what albums are out there. Murray has high awareness of music, so he can access hundreds of great songs—he knows what to look for and what to buy. His awareness is great, and, therefore, so is his access. When you compare my library of tunes and Murray's, mine's embarrassing and his is extraordinary.

Just because you are aware of something, however, doesn't mean you will *always* be able to access it. Anywhere Leaders may have a high awareness of the resources out there, but their Anywhere Leader jobs may limit their access to those resources. When I left the stable corporate setting and found myself in the role of leading a start-up company, I realized that suddenly a lot of people had a lot less time for me. When I held a position of authority, it was easy to capture people's attention and access their time. When I was running a much smaller office on a shoestring budget, not so much.

An Anywhere Leader in an uncertain and unfamiliar environment has less access to resources that may be valuable to them in their role. The fewer resources an Anywhere Leader can access, the lower the environmental munificence of his job (see Figure 16.2).

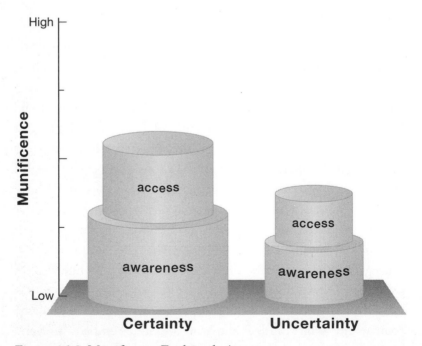

Figure 16.2 Munificence Explained: Access

Just as *awareness* serves as a base for access, so does *access* serve as a base measure for *application*—the third measure of a job's munificence. If I can access more resources, then I can apply more resources to the needs of my business. I can put whatever I can access to work. If I can access thought leaders, then I can enlist their minds to tackle a problem that others are stuck on. If I can access a good project management system, then I can deploy the system in my business to zero in on greater productivity.

Anywhere Leaders often don't have such luxuries in their jobs. Anywhere Leaders' jobs usually lack the abundance of familiar, proven, and available resources that make people feel comfortable and safe. Thus, these jobs have a lot of uncertainty (see Figure 16.3).

Lack of the right resources at the right time is just one of the dimensions used to determine whether an environment requires an Anywhere Leader's abilities. But before we move on to the next

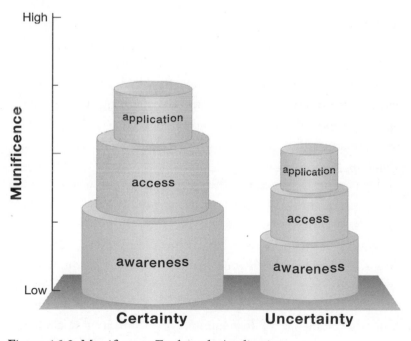

Figure 16.3 Munificence Explained: Application

dimension, take a moment to assess the munificence of your current job: Are you in a place where you have developed a perfect understanding of the resources that are available to you? Can you easily access the best knowledge, talents, and tools and apply them freely to your business needs? If your answer to either of these questions is no, then you may be in a job of uncertainty—a job for an Anywhere Leader. To know for sure, you'll need to consider these further measures.

Environmental Dynamism

It just makes sense that a word like "dynamism" would be one of the factors we'd use to measure environmental uncertainty. Dynamism represents movement, force, and energy. Dynamism is the opposite of lethargy. It seems like there should be a superhero named Captain Dynamic, with a big lightning bolt on his chest. The word represents a vigorous quality—being strong, spirited, and healthy.

You know those dynamic environments: the Apples, Googles, and DreamWorks . . . just to name a few. These highly energetic companies don't merely drive change; they hunger for it. They are spirited organizations that are constantly pushing the next paradigm. Because of the dynamic world they create, the people in those organizations feel the thrill (and the fear) of that ever-changing environment.

Dynamism is one of the things that gives Anywhere Leaders the intrinsic thrill they get from their work. Anywhere Leaders can put up with lower munificence because they experience high dynamism. Dynamism is what attracts Anywhere Leaders to Anywhere Leader jobs. If your organization is low in munificence and low in dynamism, it's likely not a very attractive company for any leader. The challenge presented by low dynamism is different from the challenge of low munificence—but it is a challenge nonetheless.

As with environmental munificence, an Anywhere Leader can assess her job's overall level of uncertainty by looking at three key environmental dynamism factors: *velocity*, *volatility*, and *variance*.

Let's start with *velocity*. Organizations operating at high speeds are the same organizations where uncertainty blossoms. Blinding speed is the natural pace of business for them and, if managed well, it provides a powerful competitive advantage. Leaders in these fast-moving companies must be able to process needs quickly and implement change more quickly than others. Because of the speed of business, these organizations don't have the luxury of spending six months building a long-term business strategy. For them, a strategic initiative can be designed and rolled out within a few days, not a few months—giving them a competitive advantage through their speed-to-market abilities.

On February 9, 2010, Google announced it was launching Google Buzz—a social networking and messaging tool for gmail users. The official launch of Google Buzz happened the very evening of the announcement. Within fifty-six hours of its launch, over nine million posts had been made on Google Buzz. Google wasn't looking for a slow, controlled burn. It wanted to ignite an explosion.

Some of you may be thinking that operating with such speed could be irresponsible and even dangerous. That's precisely the point. Speed—velocity—introduces a high degree of uncertainty. The slower a business moves, the more certain it can be. But Anywhere Leaders know that operating under complete certainty can also put you in the back of the pack of competition. Anywhere Leaders are OK operating with the increased uncertainty brought about by the need for speed.

The second factor in determining environmental dynamism is *volatility*. Volatility represents the unpredictable nature of an organization or an industry. Is there a more volatile industry right now than the health care industry? Health care is shifting and adjusting at a rapid pace due to new regulations, massive health care reform, an aging population with growing health care needs, and a short supply of qualified professionals. The entire health care system is changing. Physicians are no longer able to focus entirely on their craft in a small clinical environment. Now these physicians and their clinic managers are being asked to lead within a highly complex hospital system. Such a shift requires a fresh and adaptable mindset from health care leaders. In fact, health care workers are going to have to be some of the most adaptable workers for many years to come—maybe forever. These workers will be forced to effectively navigate through such volatility—through such uncertainty. It's hard to predict exactly what is in store for the health care industry because there are so many factors at work in the pursuit of health care reform when health care is already stretched and strapped.

Of course, the health care field isn't alone in its volatility. Because of globalization, other organizations and industries are growing more volatile. Economic conditions are in constant flux, because every economy has become intimately tied to every other economy around the globe. A few decades ago, what happened in Spain really didn't matter much to U.S. economics. Today, what happens in Spain is broadcast on an international platform within minutes, and Wall Street reacts. And this is a pattern that isn't likely to change in the near future. As more and more companies continue the transition to the global arena, the volatile nature of conducting business is expected to keep growing.

The third factor in determining environmental dynamism is *variance*. Variance represents the diversity of decisions and actions needed to accommodate the volatility of the job. The more volatility or unpredictability that exists in your organization, the more a broad pool of skills and talents are required to overcome that uncertainty. An organization that experiences lots of sudden change requires continuous evaluation, adjustment, and action. The reality is that good decisions and best practices don't always have a long shelf life in high-paced companies. What works today may be completely unproductive—maybe even counterproductive—tomorrow. One day a profit strategy is the smart move for your organization; then suddenly a new market opens up, and a volume strategy is the only way to capture market share quickly—asking for new skill sets.

Last year at SVI, our organization was focused on a deployment strategy for e-learning products. We wanted to own the platform for launching e-learning modules in volume. As we pursued this strategy, we realized that we were unable to keep up with the developing technology. We had a choice: to be bullheaded about our decision to launch our own platform and remain steadfast, or to change our strategy to focus more on creating great e-learning content while leveraging the new and exciting technology being developed by others. Fortunately, we weren't bullheaded. We shifted our strategy. Some people would call this inconsistent. We think it was smarter to diverge from our original plan—to come up with a new and better plan—in order to maximize our market penetration. To vary was the right call, and it helped us adjust appropriately to the opportunity.

Rapid change is responsible for lowering the shelf life of our decisions. Our actions just don't have quite the staying power that they once did. Uncertainty forces us to bring a broader base of decisions or actions to our business. The fact that we can't so easily predict future obstacles means that we must be able to adjust—varying from our original plan and going in a completely new direction, even when it may be perceived as inconsistent.

Before moving on to the last dimension of environmental uncertainty, take a moment to assess the dynamism of your current job:

- Is your business constantly shifting and adjusting?

- Do you get a thrill out of the velocity and volatility of your business?

- Are you having to bring a broader base of decisions
  and actions to your role?

If you can answer yes to these three questions, then it's likely that you are an Anywhere Leader in a job that only an Anywhere Leader can successfully fill.

Now let's take a look at the final measure of environmental uncertainty.

Environmental Complexity

A complex environment is an uncertain one. Complex organizations are fairly easy to define; this has been done, for example, in the works of Charles Perrow, author of *Complex Organizations*. He argues that when people think of complex organizations, they think of companies with sophisticated processes, structures, and strategies. This definition works, but maybe there's more to it. Who among us is part of an organization that isn't in some way, shape, or form a shining example of sophisticated politics, complicated procedures, and unwritten codes? But businesses, like people, vary dramatically. Some organizations are only slightly complex—they take only a handful of weeks to understand and less than a year to master. Other organizations are so complex that you can spend an entire career at one of them and still not understand all of the nuances.

So what makes one job more complex than another? First, we experience greater complexity in our roles within our business when we have lots of aggressive and capable competitors. Second, the complexity of our business increases in proportion to our level of responsibility, adding more pressure to the performance expectations. The more responsibility we have, the more complex our job is. Last, complexity grows when we have a multifaceted and complicated workload. Complexity increases uncertainty because it introduces more factors to try to manage and control. As in the previous sections, to easily categorize and recall these factors, I've split them into three categories: *market, mixture,* and *multiples.*

Let's start with the *market.* Your market is defined by your customers and your competitors: what are you selling, who are you selling it to, and who is out there trying to outsell you. For SVI, the market is middle- to large-sized, highly complex organizations who want to buy organizational development solutions that help increase the impact and engagement of their workforce. We have lots of competitors around the globe, but not nearly so many as do health care companies or consumer packaged goods companies. My market isn't nearly so competitive as the market for commercial air travel. When lots of competitors are vying for limited consumer dollars, a market is more complex—and uncertain. Here's a piece of advice: don't open up another coffee or donut shop in Manhattan. It's a saturated market.

The more saturated your market, the more adjustments are needed to stay ahead of the competition. A more saturated market requires more creativity. A saturated market with aggressive competitors forces more pressure on price from consumers, leading to tighter margins that must be more tightly managed. The stakes are higher in such a competitive environment because there's no grace for a wrong move. Your competitors, like piranhas, are out there waiting to attack.

If your market is full of fierce competitors vying for limited consumer dollars, then your market is adding to the complexity of your business.

The second factor in determining complexity is the *mixture*— that is, the diversity of our products and the diversity of our marketplace. I have a good friend who works for Ghirardelli Chocolate Company. He loves his job—who wouldn't? Ghirardelli is a really cool company that makes a great product. This company focuses on one thing—chocolate—and they do chocolate very well. They don't have a significant amount of diversity in their product offering; this adds simplicity to their business model. Contrast

214 The Anywhere Leader

Ghirardelli with Nestlé, which has over six thousand brands that compete in the beverage category as well as the baby food and pet foods category. Nestlé has a very diverse product mix, so their business environment is more complex than Ghirardelli's.

Additionally, Nestlé operates in eighty-six different countries, whereas Ghirardelli operates in one: the United States. The marketplace for Ghirardelli is not nearly as diverse—and therefore not nearly as complex—as the highly diverse marketplace in which Nestlé operates. Nestlé is forced to manage many more factors than Ghirardelli is forced to manage. Both Nestlé's and Ghirardelli's strategies in product mix and marketplace are by design, but in Ghirardelli's case, the design is for an intense focus on one product category, so it is less complex than the Nestlé model. To be a leader at Nestlé is to deal with more uncertainty in your operations than you'd face as a leader at Ghirardelli—by virtue of the larger market and more complicated mixture of products.

For the sake of alliteration, I've named the third factor in determining environmental complexity *multiples*. It represents the many responsibilities in a business, a division, a team, or a leadership role. The more responsibility a job places on an individual, the greater the complexity and uncertainty of that person's working world. When I committed to writing this book, I didn't simply accept that responsibility and shun my other responsibilities at SVI. The workload was going to have to increase—same job as before, then add five months to write about sixty thousand words while continuing to capture more and more data from research. Suddenly a host of doubts came to mind. *Can I manage the workload? Can I spend enough time with our clients? Can I be involved in the business enough? Will I have time to invest in my staff?* These were important questions, but before I committed to writing the book, the answer had always been a resounding yes. Now my confidence was a little shaky. I wasn't quite so sure as I'd been before—these added responsibilities made my world more complex, more uncertain.

When multiple responsibilities and more accountability are added to the already crowded plates of business leaders, they are forced to manage more at once. A twenty-year manager of a local grocery store deals with far less complexity than a global vice president responsible for operations in eighty-six countries. Sure, the vice president has a larger staff, but the larger responsibilities and multifaceted nature of the role force her to observe, juggle, and manage an enormous number of factors that are difficult to control yet have a significant impact on organizational performance. This is the kind of job that demands the capabilities of an Anywhere Leader.

Are you in an Anywhere Leader job? Or do you have your eyes on a job and want to know how big a role uncertainty plays in it? Ask yourself these key questions as you attempt to assess whether your job environment is right for you:

- Is it clear whether or not you'll have easy access to the resources necessary for this job, if and when you need them?

- Are people in your job operating quickly, maybe even frantically, and having to regularly adapt to unexpected twists and turns?

- Does your job require you to multitask and juggle responsibilities in a high-risk, high-accountability?

In summary, a job for an Anywhere Leader is one that features uncertainty—the unfamiliar, the unknown, and the unpredictable nature of business. Maybe you're an Anywhere Leader wondering whether you're in one of those jobs. Maybe you're an aspiring Anywhere Leader who wants to evaluate the next career pursuit. Maybe you're an organizational manager trying to determine whether a new position calls for an Anywhere Leader.

If you're like me, then you've probably read up to this point and captured some helpful information that will equip you to lead effectively in today's business environment. But if you're like me, you're also wondering how in the world you're going to grow in all the ways suggested in this book and pull off all of the recommendations as well. After all, we are all already loaded to the gills. We don't have room for much else.

That's what the next chapter is for. Chapter Seventeen will focus on how to weave Anywhere Leader traits and strengths into your current structure. We will do that not by asking you to add a few things, but by asking you to change a few things. You will learn how to adopt Anywhere Leader traits without anyone asking you to do more on top of everything else you already have to do. Read on to see how to restructure your life to live as an Anywhere Leader.

Note

1. See G. G. Dess and D. W. Beard, "Dimensions of Organizational Task Environments," *Administrative Science Quarterly*, Vol. 29, No. 1, 52–73 (Cornell, 1984).

17

RESTRUCTURE YOUR LIFE FOR TRANSPORTABILITY

It's time to embrace the new ways of working. In fact, it's a little past the ideal time. If you're just starting to work in the new world, then you've got some catching up to do. Anywhere Leaders have moved on from Effective Work Practices 1.0; they have adopted the 2.0 version—and 2.0 tools are helping them get ahead. Effective work practices for Anywhere Leaders are practices that help them sift through the raging river of knowledge, where the knowledge current is destroying the levies that are trying to contain and control it. Knowledge is growing at a rapid pace and being shared abundantly—and no one can keep up with it, though many try.

Those who are growing more and more ineffective in their leadership are either ignoring the evolution of work practices or they are trying to embrace every aspect (too much) of this evolution. Those who choose to ignore it are failing to keep up with the global conversation. Their knowledge is quickly dissipating. Then there are those leaders who are all in, quickly adopting every new technology, every new tool, and every new feature. These leaders want to be in every conversation—drinking from the informational fire hose.

So how does the Anywhere Leader lead when his capacity is limited and the knowledge conversations are boundless? How do these leaders restructure their lives and their work practices to be truly transportable—a requirement to be a valuable leader in today's complex business environment?

Get Accessible

Are you one of those 24/7 types—always plugged in and always accessible? Early in my career, I worked for the J.B. Hunt trucking company. I was told that the job never stops—that trucks are driving twenty-four hours a day and seven days a week—so I needed to be accessible all the time in case of emergencies. Even though I wasn't working all the time, I was never able to completely detach from my job. Family vacations were accompanied by the cell phone, and dinners were often interrupted. Sometimes the phone would interrupt a good dream, ringing at two or three o'clock in the morning. I prided myself in my accessibility, but complete accessibility ushered in burnout fairly quickly.

I remember making a decision on a particular vacation in Florida to leave my phone at home. I knew if I had it, I'd check emails and missed calls. For seven days I was without my phone. Those seven days were the most relaxing and rewarding I've had. I truly disconnected and recharged.

Recharging your batteries is so important for an Anywhere Leader. Why? Because so many people drain them. Anywhere Leaders put a lot of energy into their work and into others. They give away more energy than they get from others. So they get depleted. Like anyone else, when Anywhere Leaders are depleted, they aren't very effective anymore, and they certainly aren't engaged.

The point is, to be effective when you're fully accessible, you must intentionally plan for some of your time to be fully *inaccessible*. As CEO of SVI, I'm fully accessible. I carry my phone with me almost everywhere I go. I check my calendar one last time each night before I go to bed. I also check my emails and missed calls. It's not uncommon for me to make a phone call or two at night and on weekends. But I also take many vacations and section off time for being fully inaccessible. I don't try to be somewhat accessible and somewhat inaccessible at the same time. I'm either all in or all out—for a period. What are your periods of full-on accessibility? What are your periods of full-on inaccessibility?

Beyond your availability, accessibility also represents your access to others and their access to you. If you're an Anywhere Leader, then lots of people have you on their speed dial. Access is an important quality of an Anywhere Leader, because these leaders are often on the move—racing from conversation to conversation, meeting to meeting, or continent to continent. Their access keeps them informed and in the know even when they're on the run. They don't have to be there for the update— they can get the update from anywhere. Therefore, Anywhere Leaders are master mobile users. Their mobile devices are their connection to others, to data, to just-in-time training. These master mobile users learn how to get work done on a mobile interface—reviewing spreadsheets and editing documents. Presentations on the fly are being made through an Anywhere Leader's mobile device. Anywhere Leaders don't wait to get back to the office before answering an email; they answer it on the go. They are completely accessible, until they intentionally get completely inaccessible and detached for a period of time to recover—going all in for leisure, for fun, for family, and for friends.

Get Wired

Being wired means doing more to capture external knowledge. Anywhere Leaders are connected—and they set up lots of inputs. In the old days, our admired leaders held all of the knowledge within their own minds. They were smarter than others and more experienced. We put our leaders up on the podiums and listened intently as they issued their words of wisdom. They spoke, we listened, we learned. And we never questioned them. But that's not the case today.

Today, no one leader holds all of the answers. That knowledge is usually held in the crowds. Therefore, Anywhere Leaders don't overexert themselves trying to hoard all of the knowledge; rather, they reach out and network and tap into crowds—followers, peers, superiors, the company, and experts.

To effectively tap into the crowds, a leader must give the crowds a voice—even when the voice has a different opinion.

Anywhere Leaders shift their mindset from having to hold all of the answers to effectively using the knowledge of others. They are involved in cultures of collaboration where open communication is requested and people aren't intimidated to give their dissenting opinions. Anywhere Leaders give their followers permission to disagree. They seek the influence of their followers. They rely on their followers to equip them with the right knowledge for a given situation or circumstance. But not just followers—these Anywhere Leaders get feedback in open chat rooms at times. They update their blogs and appreciate any comment, good or bad, from readers.

Talk about wiring your organization for excellence! Consider IBM's "Jam" sessions. For those to whom these are not familiar, IBM created a series of online collaborative sessions designed to "serve as a spark and a catalyst for change," according to its program director. Since the project's inception, IBM has used Jam events internally to collaborate across its entire worldwide organization, allowing IBMers to contribute their thoughts and ideas. Almost 320,000 IBMers have participated in these events. Impressive, by any standards.

Get Attuned

Anywhere Leaders are extraordinary at filtering lots of information and quickly getting to the valuable information. You might say that their ability to acquire information fast attunes them more quickly to the needs and opportunities. They have established ways of wading through lots of facts, figures, and insights without getting consumed by them. These include filtering tools such as push and pull technologies. These allow Anywhere Leaders to ignore 99 percent of the information out there and receive the critical 1 percent of information that is relevant to them and their needs. They create pathways that filter and funnel relevant data from boundless information flows. These leaders don't view the entire Internet as their inbox. Push and pull technologies allow them to subscribe to specific channels of important information.

Once a user subscribes to one of these channels, the information from the channel is pushed to the subscriber either through email or through their Really Simple Syndication (RSS) feeds. Twitter is another example of push technology. By following people who hold relevant information for me, I have access to their knowledge. Their ideas are being pushed to me because I follow them. A well-tended Twitter community is a human-powered search engine that will continuously notify you of great content.

The ultimate pull technology on earth is Google. This is an educated guess, but I imagine that 90 percent of the world uses only about 5 percent of Google's search and filtering capabilities. Advanced search techniques, called operators, help users backward-engineer Google according to their needs. If you've never clicked on the "Advanced Search" link, then give it a try by searching for something very specific using the Google form. Pay attention to the text bar at the top of the form to see how Google automatically fills in the text with "operators" according to how you answer the questions. These operators can help you capture search engine shortcuts. I think you'll find your information flow to be more efficient and on target—cutting through lots of noise and clutter.

There are an enormous number of tools out there to help a leader learn how to filter information; entire books have been written on the subject. Anywhere Leaders stay up to speed on new tools and are selective in the ones they use to remain efficient and nimble. They don't seek to become technology gurus, but they do want to become experts in the tools that have the best chance of helping them capture the information that is most vital to their jobs. Are you using filtering tools to sift through boundless amounts of available knowledge? If not, start investigating. Learn what collaboration technologies can offer, sign up for a few blogs that present helpful and relevant content, access push technology for your mobile phone, and use social media. If all of this sounds intimidating to you and you just don't know where to start, then do what an Anywhere Leader does—be resourceful. Build a relationship with someone who knows and uses these tools very well and then access her knowledge. These filtering technologies are oftentimes intimidating to me and I find myself relying on a close friend of mine and fellow SVIer: the aforementioned Murray, the music connoisseur. He is a power searcher and master filterer. He helps me get set up with helpful tools, and I'm much more efficient because of it. I'm not getting lost in the noise of limitless information, and I'm protecting my time and capacity without losing my connection to valuable knowledge.

Get Un-nested

There are those people who are heavily wired and holed up in a dark room lit only by monitors. Their connection to the world happens through a computer screen. They are not Anywhere

Leaders. The fact that they are wired keeps these holed-up leaders *nested*. They don't find much reason to get up or get out because all the information is fed to them right where they are.

These holed-up leaders miss the experience. They miss the touch, the feel, and the emotion that comes from actually being there. They may watch or read the information, but they certainly don't experience it. And holed-up leaders bring no experience to the world.

Anywhere Leaders are *genchi genbutsu* leaders. *Genchi genbutsu*, made famous by Toyota's Production System, means "to go and see." Anywhere Leaders go and see. They aren't holed-up in their offices. They don't lead from behind their desks. They are up and out there, walking the halls, visiting the plants and stores, and meeting with customers and suppliers. The fact that they are wired doesn't keep them holed-up; rather, it unleashes them to tour the world—to influence and be influenced through personal interaction. They don't just see the data report of the problem; they see the problem, firsthand.

You may have heard that one of President George W. Bush's biggest regrets of his presidency was being photographed in Air Force One flying high above the devastation in New Orleans and other Gulf cities, brought about by Hurricane Katrina. When the photograph was released, people viewed the picture of President Bush and developed the perception that he was detached and uncaring. In an interview with Matt Lauer of NBC, President Bush talked about how he wished he had managed things differently. He talked about how he should have touched down in Baton Rouge, met with the governor, and walked out and said to all the affected people, "I hear you. We understand. And we're going to help the state and help the local governments with as much resources as needed." He wasn't there to interact with suffering families. He didn't look the community leaders in the eye when discussing potential solutions. In Bush's words, "I did not do that. And I paid a price for it."

Are you leading from behind your desk, or are you getting out and into the business? Are you *bound* to your monitor, or is the fact that you're wired unleashing you to go and see—to get un-nested? I hope you're pursuing the latter in both cases.

Protect Your Soul

The problem with being an Anywhere Leader is that you find yourself everywhere. When you're everywhere, you may sometimes feel like you're nowhere at all. Let's face it, being un-nested can feel kind of lonely and uncomfortable at times. My office is a whole lot nicer than the business-class middle seat on a jumbo jet. Plus, I have friends at my office whom I can connect with and who understand me. I feel detached when I sit next to a complete stranger on the plane. When I'm nested, I can go home to my family and kiss the kiddos goodnight. Those are precious times for me, and I miss them when I'm away.

It's not just about being geographically away, either. I can quickly feel out of touch even when I work in Northwest Arkansas, where I live. My work can easily consume me no matter where I am. I can be operating in a spin mode—bouncing around to various conversations, addressing various issues—and feel desperately unsettled and completely ungrounded and lost. An Anywhere Leader must structure his life to be transportable, but protect his soul (the essence of life) in the process. This sounds complicated even as I write it.

Consider this. Anywhere Leaders are un-nested "go and see" leaders who are easily accessible, wired to collect timely information, and attuned to the most relevant information in order to be most productive. None of these approaches or actions supplants their integrity. Anywhere Leaders are life-essence livers and deep souls. Their integrity is at the core of their efforts. Being un-nested has significant value, but not at the expense of your most precious relationships. Being accessible keeps you informed, but what benefit is accessibility that makes you inaccessible to the most important things in life, such as your health or your family? Being wired helps you remain at the forefront of relevant trends and increases your knowledge, but trends and knowledge should be bound by the good, right, and ethical decisions. You get the point.

How do Anywhere Leaders stay grounded in their lives' real meaning without getting sucked into spin-cycle success? Well, not to oversimplify, but these leaders plant lots of reminders in their life as they go along, to help them shun the temptation of the unethical shortcuts or the morale collapses. I'm not saying these leaders are perfect in every decision—who hasn't blown it at least a few times? But they are constantly striving to be their most ideal self with the most pure and right motives. These Anywhere Leaders are the ones carrying family photos, corporate values or heritage cards, and wrist bands that represent physical strength or religious beliefs. These Anywhere Leaders are quick to grab accountability partners who help keep their behavior in check. Even when Anywhere Leaders feel alone in the unknown and unfamiliar, they have reminder items all around them that bring to mind the things that are familiar, secure, and supportive.

Anywhere Leader Approach

Now that I've mentioned the approaches to restructuring your life toward Anywhere Leadership, allow me to present the valuable outcomes of these approaches for the Anywhere Leader through the model shown in Figure 17.1.

Accessible, *wired*, *attuned*, and *un-nested* represent the leadership approaches taken by Anywhere Leaders in order to be transportable—to be able to lead effectively, anywhere and everywhere they are. Now notice the outcomes created by combining pairs of the approaches.

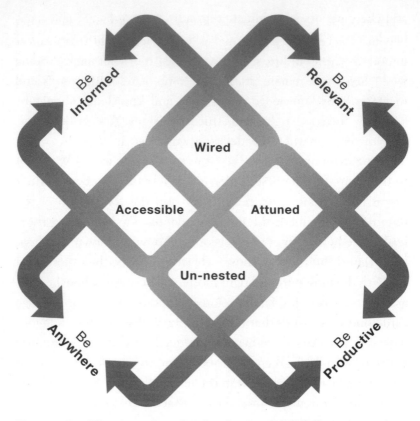

Figure 17.1 The Anywhere Leader Approach Model

An Anywhere Leader works at being un-nested. When she is also accessible, she can be anywhere she needs to be. She can be at a team rally in Vegas or a board meeting in Amsterdam, with an important customer in Atlanta or at her daughter's piano recital back home. She can leave her office to walk the halls and conduct surprise pop-ins to catch up on the lives of her employees.

I'm reminded again of my work for the J.B. Hunt trucking company. I was fortunate to be there while Mr. Hunt was still alive. He had a beautiful executive office on the top floor of corporate headquarters, but he didn't spend much time there. Mr. Hunt spent a lot of time walking the halls. Almost every afternoon around three o'clock he would walk by my cubicle, pat me on the shoulder, and cheer me on. Mr. Hunt is a business Hall of Famer and I was barely a peon. The attention he showed me was energizing and memorable. Mr. Hunt was everywhere and anywhere he needed to be. He epitomized un-nested and accessible leadership—something I have aspired to model ever since.

Un-nested + Accessible = Be Anywhere

Anywhere Leaders' accessibility helps them stay connected to people who hold valuable information. But when they're accessible to others *and* wired to informational tools and technologies, then they stay informed not just through their relationships, but also through the crowds and the thought leaders who are harder to connect to. I don't personally know many *Harvard Business Review* (HBR) contributors, but I still learn a great deal from them because I'm wired to *HBR*. I can get it on my computer or on my phone or when the magazine shows up on my desk. I've set *HBR* to be information that is pushed to me on a continuous basis. When I'm accessible to people I depend on and who sharpen me and advise me, and when I'm wired to helpful information that is pushed to me through any number of tools, then I'm well informed.

Accessible + Wired = Be Informed

I say no to probably 90 percent of the wired information that tries to make me a subscriber or user. I've found that 90 percent is irrelevant. But that remaining 10 percent is extremely valuable to me and relevant to my business. I can opt in to the truly vital information and leave the rest aside. And that's what is meant by an Anywhere Leader's being attuned. They aren't just wired to lots of information; they are able to filter it, making sure the incoming information is in tune with their needs. The fact that Anywhere Leaders are attuned makes them selective—opting in to only the relevant information, not wide open to an abundance of information that quickly becomes overwhelming.

Wired + Attuned = Be Relevant

When a leader is attuned and connected to the most relevant information and that leader is also free to go out into the business and see for herself, then she is most productive and most effective. Her leadership benefits from all the right knowledge, and the team sees her value. Because of her knowledge and her visibility, she can personally connect with others and ignite their charge to action. Anywhere Leaders need to be seen and need to be in the know. Being attuned may make you knowledgeable. But knowledge alone won't make you productive. An Anywhere Leader puts the knowledge to work—and into action—through people. And any time people are involved, making the connection with them is important if you're going to move them and help them be productive. You connect better when you understand their world.

Attuned + Un-nested = Be Productive

Anywhere Leaders take all four approaches to pull off successes in uncertain situations and unfamiliar environments. And they do it without losing their soul, their integrity, and the essence of their life.

Closing

If I have any concern about this book, it's the concern that you will interpret *The Anywhere Leader* as having little relevancy beyond today's best leadership practices for trying to succeed in these complex and tough economic times. As the writer, to have my message so interpreted would make me feel shallow. My purpose in writing this was much deeper; it came about as I watched many friends transition out of roles and suddenly find themselves in unfamiliar territory, not knowing what to do or what lay ahead of them. I could see many of those friends deal with the significant stress of sudden change, having no ability to predict what was about to happen to them and their future.

Losing my first son to leukemia disrupted my life significantly. I learned that life is short and precious. So when my friends and acquaintances are forced to deal with disruption, I dream of a magic wand that makes everything right for them when they wake up in the morning so they can get started living life abundantly. As we all know, no such wand exists. Writing about ways to help others deal with uncertainty seemed like the next best thing.

I recently watched the movie *Up in the Air*, featuring George Clooney as an executive named Ryan Bingham who traveled the world as a consultant and helped companies downsize their workforces. He had accumulated ten million air miles from his travels around the world, and he claimed his true home was the very airports he frequented. He made good money, ate good dinners, and traveled to some great cities to do a very tough, but necessary job. In essence, he disrupted people's lives. Bingham was tough and emotionless at the beginning of the movie, but gained his soul as he battled a few personal challenges and gained a few "Aha!" moments. Some might claim that Bingham was an Anywhere Leader because he was constantly on the move. Sure, Bingham was chalking up a significant amount of air miles. But he was no Anywhere Leader.

Why? Because Bingham wasn't driven for progress—he was driven to accumulate those air miles and live a life with no strings attached. Bingham wasn't curious; he always came with the answers, but never with a desire to discover and learn. When Bingham traveled, he was blind to life and culture around him. For Bingham, life wasn't the big deal—lifestyle was. Bingham was far from resourceful, because he had little imagination and he certainly wasn't inclusive of others. He worked hard to make sure his life was perfectly organized and predictable. And yes, it was a movie—because we all know life is never organized and predictable.

Our lives are going to include many disruptions. For those of you who are already Anywhere Leaders—who found this book

more of a review of your best qualities than a blueprint for more—
you should be confident that you have the right traits and tools to
deal with those disruptions. But for those of you who gleaned new
insight from these pages, rest assured: by adopting Anywhere
Leader traits and behaviors, you can grow personally and professionally. In learning how to better handle the uncertainty of work
and life, you can become a stronger leader and contributor to your
business, to your community, and to society.

A tall order, I know. But a worthy pursuit.

Onward!

ACKNOWLEDGMENTS

The biggest reward I get from writing this book is how much I've been able to learn from so many brilliant people. I'm also humbled by and extremely appreciative of everyone who has supported me in the process.

My wife, Mel, has been my biggest champion, my strongest supporter, my encourager, and the enabler of everything I do.

My children, Alex and Jax, were my release and my breath of fresh air throughout this project.

Trevor King, SVI's thought leader, dedicated hundreds of hours confirming and improving the concepts of the book and expanding my thinking. This book would not have been possible without his significant input and influence.

My business partners, Autumn Manning, Tim Harmon, and Erin Fritsche, took over so many of my responsibilities as SVI's CEO, giving me the capacity to invest the necessary time in completing this book.

The entire SVI team has been my inspiration through this entire process. Their dedication to our mission is unmatchable.

Herb Schaffner, my agent, has been a valuable adviser and has helped navigate this project effectively to completion.

Gail Belsky provided vital editorial advice through much of the project.

Susan Williams, my cditor at Jossey-Bass, has helped me elevate the value of this book to the reader and position it well in the marketplace.

Finally, I would like to thank the clients of SVI. We are blessed to work with some of the world's greatest organizations. It's through our partnership with them that I get to see Anywhere Leaders in action every day.

ABOUT THE AUTHOR

M ike Thompson is a two-time author and the CEO of SVI, a leading organizational development company whose mission is to create irresistible companies and extraordinary people. Mike is one of the most forward thinkers in leadership today. He coaches current and next-generation executives at many of the world's largest companies to support them in developing sustainable and scalable organizational development solutions.

Mike holds a master's degree in leadership and ethics from John Brown University, serves on the executive board of directors for The Center for Retailing Excellence, and has received numerous recognitions, including the Business of the Year award and the 40 Under 40 Award in his home state. Prior to founding SVI, Mike was the founder and president of ThompsonMurray, now Saatchi & Saatchi X, a leader in in-store marketing.

Serving six years in the Air Force and Air National Guard as a life support technician, Mike instructed military personnel in land and water survival and evasion.

Mike lives in Arkansas with his wife, Mel, and their two children, Alex and Jax.

INDEX